Leadership Thinking 101 - The Art of Strategic Minds

Mohd Arif

Outline:

Preface:

Leadership Thinking 101 - The Art of Strategic Minds

Dear Reader,

Welcome to "Leadership Thinking 101: The Art of Strategic Minds." This book is a journey into the fascinating realm of leadership and the profound impact of thinking strategically in the pursuit of excellence. Whether you're an aspiring leader, a seasoned professional, or simply intrigued by the art of leadership, this book aims to provide you with valuable insights, practical tools, and a deeper understanding of the strategic mindset that drives exceptional leaders.

The world of leadership is ever-evolving, and as we navigate an increasingly complex and interconnected global landscape, the need for effective leadership has never been more critical. Great leaders possess the ability to envision a brighter future, inspire those around them, and make decisions that shape the course of history. But what lies beneath the surface of their successes? What thought processes and cognitive abilities enable them to lead with distinction?

In "Leadership Thinking 101," we delve into the core essence of leadership thinking. Our journey begins with understanding the very concept of leadership thinking and its significance in personal and professional contexts. We explore the theories that underpin effective leadership and the role of emotional intelligence in guiding leaders towards success.

One of the cornerstones of this book is the exploration of strategic minds. We dissect the elements that constitute a strategic thinker, from vision and adaptability to critical thinking and problem-solving prowess. Through real-life examples and case studies, we aim to illustrate the profound impact of strategic minds on shaping organizations, communities, and the world at large.

Decision-making is a critical aspect of leadership, and we dedicate an entire chapter to dissecting the various decision-making strategies employed by effective leaders. We also address the impact of cognitive biases on leadership decisions and offer practical techniques to enhance judgment and discernment.

Effective communication is another vital aspect of leadership thinking. We delve into the art of persuasive communication, fostering meaningful connections, and influencing others positively. Our goal is to equip you with communication skills that amplify your leadership impact and resonate with your audience.

Leadership is a journey of personal growth and transformation. Throughout the book, we emphasize the importance of cultivating a leadership mindset, embracing a growth-oriented approach, and learning from challenges to emerge as resilient and visionary leaders.

Ethics and integrity are at the heart of exceptional leadership. We explore the moral dimensions of leadership thinking, underscoring the significance of transparency, trust, and ethical decision-making in leadership roles. The inclusion of ethical case studies sheds light on the dilemmas leaders face and the ethical considerations that guide their actions.

Leading teams is a hallmark of leadership, and in this book, we provide valuable insights into the dynamics of team leadership, collaboration, and motivation. By exploring team-based scenarios, we help you navigate the challenges and opportunities that arise when leading a group of diverse individuals towards a common goal.

Lastly, we address the art of navigating change and uncertainty. As leaders, we encounter an ever-changing landscape, and the ability to adapt and embrace uncertainty becomes paramount. This chapter provides strategies for leading through change and leveraging uncertainty as a catalyst for growth.

At its core, "Leadership Thinking 101: The Art of Strategic Minds" seeks to empower you with knowledge, inspiration, and practical tools that can elevate your leadership potential. Our hope is that this book sparks introspection, ignites your passion for leadership, and empowers you to make a positive impact in your personal and professional endeavors.

We sincerely thank you for embarking on this journey with us, and we hope that the insights and lessons within these pages will serve as a guiding light on your path to becoming a strategic and impactful leader.

With warmest regards,

Mohd Arif

Author, "Leadership Thinking 101: The Art of Strategic Minds"

Introduction:

Leadership Thinking 101 - The Art of Strategic Minds

In the realm of leadership, there exists an enigmatic force that propels individuals to rise above challenges, inspire greatness in others, and shape the course of history. This force is the art of strategic minds - a profound way of thinking that empowers leaders to navigate complexity, envision the future, and make decisions that lead to remarkable achievements.

Welcome to "Leadership Thinking 101: The Art of Strategic Minds." In this book, we embark on a journey into the heart of leadership thinking, exploring the cognitive processes, qualities, and approaches that define exceptional leaders. Whether you're a seasoned leader seeking to enhance your skills or an aspiring leader with a thirst for knowledge, this exploration of leadership thinking is designed to equip you with the tools needed to excel in your leadership journey.

The world we inhabit is in a constant state of transformation. Technological advancements, global connectivity, and societal shifts have reshaped the landscape in which leaders operate. In such a dynamic environment, leadership demands more than just traditional authority; it requires a strategic mindset that can anticipate challenges, seize opportunities, and inspire innovation.

Understanding Leadership Thinking

Our journey begins with an in-depth examination of leadership thinking. We will explore the fundamental theories that underpin leadership styles and the cognitive processes that guide decision-making. Understanding the intricacies of leadership thinking lays the foundation for becoming a more effective and insightful leader.

The Elements of Strategic Minds

To be a strategic thinker is to possess a unique set of attributes that elevate leadership to new heights. We delve into the essential elements of strategic minds, from the power of visionary thinking to the flexibility required to adapt in ever-changing circumstances. Critical thinking, problem-solving acumen, and long-term planning are just a few of the aspects that form the backbone of strategic leadership.

Decisions That Define Leadership

Leaders are often faced with pivotal moments that define their trajectories. In this section, we explore the art of decision-making and the methodologies leaders employ to navigate complex choices. Unraveling the influence of cognitive biases and honing the ability to make well-informed decisions are crucial steps toward mastering the art of strategic minds.

Communication and Influence

An effective leader is not only a strategic thinker but also a skilled communicator. Communication is the bridge that connects leaders with their teams, stakeholders, and the wider world. We delve into the art of persuasive communication, active listening, and the profound impact of influential leadership.

Developing a Leadership Mindset

A strategic mindset is not innate; it is a product of personal growth and continuous learning. In this chapter, we emphasize the importance of cultivating a leadership mindset, embracing challenges as opportunities for growth, and developing resilience in the face of adversity.

Ethics and Integrity in Leadership

Leadership carries a moral responsibility. Ethical considerations and integrity are cornerstones of effective leadership. We delve into the ethical dimensions of leadership thinking and explore case studies of leaders who exemplify ethical decision-making.

Leading Teams with a Strategic Mind

Great leaders are not solitary figures but visionaries who inspire teams to work cohesively towards shared goals. We discuss the dynamics of team leadership, fostering collaboration, and empowering team members to unleash their full potential.

Navigating Change and Uncertainty

In an ever-changing world, adaptability and embracing uncertainty are indispensable traits for leaders. This section provides strategies for leading through change, seizing opportunities amidst uncertainty, and charting a course for success.

As we embark on this exploration of leadership thinking, our goal is to empower you with knowledge, inspiration, and practical wisdom. This book is not a prescription for leadership; rather, it is a guide that encourages you to embrace your unique leadership journey and discover the art of strategic minds within yourself.

We hope that "Leadership Thinking 101: The Art of Strategic Minds" sparks curiosity, prompts introspection, and inspires you to make a positive impact in the spheres where leadership thrives. Let us begin this transformative journey into the heart of leadership thinking together.

With anticipation and excitement,

Leadership thinking refers to the cognitive processes, mindset, and approach that effective leaders adopt to navigate challenges, make decisions, and influence others. It encompasses a range of mental abilities and qualities that enable leaders to envision a compelling future, devise strategies, and inspire individuals and teams to work collaboratively towards achieving common goals.

In personal contexts, leadership thinking plays a pivotal role in guiding individuals to take charge of their lives, set meaningful goals, and lead themselves towards personal growth and success. It involves self-awareness, emotional intelligence, and the ability to make wise decisions that align with one's values and aspirations.

In professional contexts, leadership thinking is critical for individuals in managerial, executive, and leadership roles. It goes beyond traditional authority and focuses on leading by example, building strong relationships, and creating a positive work environment. Leadership thinking is essential for setting a clear vision for the organization, crafting strategies to achieve objectives, and mobilizing teams to work towards a common purpose.

The significance of leadership thinking in personal and professional contexts lies in its ability to:

1. Drive Vision and Direction: Leadership thinking empowers individuals to see beyond the present and envision a future that aligns with their values and aspirations. Leaders with a strategic mindset can set a clear vision and communicate it effectively to inspire others.

2. Foster Decision-Making: In both personal and professional realms, leaders are frequently faced with complex decisions. Leadership thinking equips individuals with the ability to analyze situations, consider multiple perspectives, and make informed choices that lead to positive outcomes.

3. Inspire and Motivate: Leaders who think strategically have a profound influence on their teams and stakeholders. Their ability to communicate effectively, empathize with others, and demonstrate integrity can inspire and motivate individuals to give their best efforts towards shared goals.

4. Promote Innovation and Adaptability: In a rapidly changing world, leadership thinking is crucial for fostering innovation and adaptability. Strategic leaders encourage creativity, embrace change, and lead their organizations through transitions with agility and resilience.

5. Build High-Performing Teams: Leadership thinking involves understanding the strengths and weaknesses of team members and aligning their skills towards achieving collective success. Leaders who prioritize collaboration and empowerment can build cohesive and high-performing teams.

6. Cultivate Ethical Leadership: Ethical considerations are fundamental in leadership thinking. Leaders with strong ethical foundations prioritize fairness, honesty, and integrity, thereby earning the trust and respect of their followers.

7. Promote Continuous Growth: Leadership thinking encourages continuous learning and personal development. Leaders who invest in their growth and encourage the growth of others create a culture of continuous improvement within organizations.

Overall, leadership thinking is a dynamic and multifaceted aspect of effective leadership. It empowers individuals to become visionary, empathetic, and strategic leaders who can create a positive and lasting impact both in their personal lives and in the organizations they lead.

In the realm of leadership, an extraordinary trait sets exceptional leaders apart from the rest - the possession of a strategic mind. Strategic minds encompass a distinct set of cognitive abilities, forward-thinking vision, and problem-solving acumen that enable leaders to navigate complex challenges, capitalize on opportunities, and steer their organizations towards success.

As we embark on this exploration of strategic minds and its relation to effective leadership, we dive into the essence of what makes a leader truly exceptional. The concept of strategic minds goes beyond the traditional understanding of leadership and delves into the heart of what it takes to be a visionary, influential, and adaptive leader in today's dynamic and interconnected world.

Understanding Strategic Minds

At its core, a strategic mind is one that possesses the capacity to think beyond the immediate circumstances and envision a future that aligns with a clear and compelling vision. Strategic thinkers exhibit an acute awareness of the ever-changing landscape, anticipate potential obstacles, and devise robust plans that capitalize on emerging opportunities.

The essence of strategic minds lies not only in their ability to craft innovative solutions but also in their capacity to discern the most prudent course of action amidst a myriad of possibilities. These leaders see the big picture while simultaneously attending to the finer details, striking a delicate balance that propels their organizations towards sustainable growth and success.

The Synergy of Strategic Minds and Effective Leadership

Effective leadership demands more than traditional management skills. Leaders with strategic minds have the ability to inspire and motivate their teams, communicate a compelling vision, and make decisions that are guided by data and wisdom rather than impulsivity. This unique combination of qualities empowers leaders to chart a course for their organizations, align their teams towards a common purpose, and embrace change with confidence and adaptability.

Strategic minds in leadership are not limited to top executives or CEOs; they can be found at all levels of an organization. Whether leading a small team or an entire company, strategic thinkers bring an innovative and forward-thinking approach to their roles, driving success and resilience even in the face of uncertainty.

The Journey Ahead

As we delve deeper into the concept of strategic minds and its interplay with effective leadership, this book seeks to equip you with the knowledge, insights, and practical tools needed to cultivate and leverage strategic thinking in your leadership journey. We will explore the key components of strategic minds, delve into the decision-making processes that underpin effective leadership, and discover how strategic thinkers communicate, inspire, and navigate change.

Through real-life examples, case studies, and actionable advice, we hope to ignite your passion for leadership, inspire you to develop your strategic mindset, and enable you to create a lasting impact in your personal and professional endeavors.

The road to becoming a strategic leader is both challenging and rewarding, but the journey starts with understanding the concept of strategic minds and embracing the principles that drive exceptional leadership. Let us embark on this transformative exploration together, as we uncover the art of strategic minds and its profound impact on effective leadership.

Chapter 1: Understanding Leadership Thinking

Introduction

Leadership, at its essence, is not just a title or a position; it is a way of thinking. In this chapter, we delve into the depths of leadership thinking, exploring the theories, concepts, and psychological foundations that underpin the mindset of effective leaders. Understanding the nuances of leadership thinking is the first step towards becoming a more insightful, empathetic, and strategic leader in personal and professional contexts.

1.1 The Essence of Leadership Thinking

To comprehend leadership thinking, we must go beyond the surface and explore the core principles that guide the thought processes of exceptional leaders. We examine how leadership thinking transcends the boundaries of authority and hierarchy, fostering an environment where collaboration, innovation, and shared vision thrive.

Leadership thinking lies at the heart of effective leadership. It goes beyond mere actions or decisions; it is the foundational mindset that shapes how leaders perceive the world, approach challenges, and inspire others to achieve shared goals. In this section, we delve into the essence of leadership thinking, exploring its core characteristics and the broader impact it has on individuals, teams, and organizations.

1. Understanding Beyond Authority

At its core, leadership thinking is not bound by traditional notions of authority or hierarchical structures. It is a way of thinking that transcends titles and positions, empowering individuals to lead from any level within an organization. Leadership thinking embraces the idea that anyone can make a positive impact and influence change, regardless of their official role.

2. Visionary and Future-Oriented

Leadership thinking is inherently visionary and future-oriented. Strategic leaders possess the ability to envision possibilities beyond the present realities. They paint a compelling picture of the future, inspiring their teams to work collaboratively towards that shared vision. This forward-looking mindset enables leaders to chart a course for success, even amidst uncertainty and rapid change.

3. Inclusive and Collaborative

Effective leadership thinking involves inclusivity and collaboration. Strategic leaders recognize the diverse strengths and perspectives of their team members and actively seek input from all stakeholders. They foster an environment of trust and openness, where everyone's voice is valued, leading to innovative solutions and higher team engagement.

4. Learning and Adaptability

Leadership thinking is a continuous learning process. Strategic leaders embrace challenges as opportunities for growth and view failures as stepping stones to success. They are adaptable, capable of adjusting their strategies based on new information and changing circumstances. This adaptability ensures that leaders remain agile and responsive in dynamic environments.

5. Strategic Decision-Making

Strategic decision-making is a hallmark of leadership thinking. Leaders analyze situations from multiple angles, weigh potential risks and rewards, and consider long-term implications before making informed choices. Their decisions are driven by a combination of data, intuition, and critical thinking, aligning with their vision and organizational goals.

6. Emotional Intelligence and Empathy

Leadership thinking involves emotional intelligence and empathy. Understanding and managing emotions, both their own and those of others, allows leaders to build authentic connections and foster a positive work culture. Empathy enables leaders to understand the needs and concerns of their team members, paving the way for effective communication and collaboration.

7. Resilience and Integrity

Strategic leaders exhibit resilience and integrity. They demonstrate unwavering commitment to their values and principles, even in challenging circumstances. Their integrity builds trust and credibility, enabling them to lead by example and inspire others to act ethically and responsibly.

8. Impact on Organizational Culture

Leadership thinking has a profound impact on organizational culture. When leaders embrace strategic thinking, it permeates throughout the organization, encouraging a culture of innovation, adaptability, and continuous improvement. A positive leadership mindset fosters employee engagement and loyalty, leading to higher productivity and overall organizational success.

Conclusion

The essence of leadership thinking lies in the amalgamation of visionary foresight, empathy, strategic decision-making, and adaptability. Leaders who embrace this mindset go beyond the realms of conventional leadership and inspire transformative change. As we proceed through this exploration of leadership thinking, we will delve deeper into its components and their significance in shaping effective leadership in both personal and professional contexts. By understanding the essence of leadership thinking, we pave the way for a richer and more impactful leadership journey ahead.

1.2 Theories of Leadership

Leadership theories provide valuable insights into the various approaches to leadership thinking. We explore classic and contemporary theories, such as transformational, situational, and servant leadership, understanding how they shape leaders' mindsets and influence their interactions with others.

Leadership is a complex and multifaceted phenomenon, and numerous theories have been developed over the years to understand and explain the dynamics of effective leadership. In this section, we explore some of the key theories of leadership that have shaped our understanding of leadership thinking and its impact on individuals and organizations.

1. Trait Theory of Leadership

The trait theory of leadership, which emerged in the early 20th century, posits that effective leaders possess inherent traits or qualities that set them apart from non-leaders. According to this theory, certain personality traits, such as intelligence, charisma, decisiveness, and integrity, are common among successful leaders. While trait theory laid the foundation for leadership research, it has limitations, as it oversimplifies the complex nature of leadership and does not account for situational factors.

2. Behavioral Theories of Leadership

Behavioral theories shifted the focus from inherent traits to observable behaviors exhibited by leaders. These theories suggest that leadership is a set of learned behaviors that can be taught and developed. Two prominent behavioral theories are the Ohio State Studies and the University of Michigan Studies. The Ohio State Studies identified two key leadership behaviors: initiating structure (task-oriented) and consideration (relationship-oriented). The University of Michigan Studies categorized leadership behaviors as employee-centered and job-centered.

3. Contingency Theories of Leadership

Contingency theories propose that effective leadership depends on the interaction between the leader's traits or behaviors and the specific situation or context in which they operate. The most well-known contingency theory is Fiedler's Contingency Model, which suggests that a leader's effectiveness depends on the match between their leadership style (task-oriented or relationship-oriented) and the favorability of the situation.

4. Transformational Leadership Theory

The transformational leadership theory, introduced by James MacGregor Burns and later developed by Bernard M. Bass, focuses on the leader's ability to inspire and motivate followers to achieve exceptional performance. Transformational leaders encourage personal growth, challenge the status quo, and create a compelling vision that resonates with their followers. They have a profound impact on organizational culture and stimulate intrinsic motivation among their team members.

5. Situational Leadership Theory

Situational leadership theory, proposed by Paul Hersey and Kenneth Blanchard, suggests that effective leaders adapt their leadership style based on the readiness and development level of their followers. Leaders may employ a directive style for inexperienced or less competent individuals, while a supportive and empowering style is used for more capable and motivated followers.

6. Servant Leadership

Servant leadership, coined by Robert K. Greenleaf, emphasizes the leader's focus on serving the needs of others rather than pursuing personal gain or power. Servant leaders prioritize the well-being of their followers, foster collaboration, and empower others to achieve their potential. This approach emphasizes humility, empathy, and ethical decision-making.

Conclusion

Theories of leadership have evolved over time, offering diverse perspectives on what makes an effective leader. While no single theory captures the entirety of leadership thinking, they all contribute valuable insights into the complexities of leadership and the multifaceted nature of leadership thinking. As we progress in our exploration of leadership thinking, we integrate these theories, recognizing that effective leadership encompasses a combination of traits, behaviors, adaptability, and the ability to inspire and serve others. The journey to understanding leadership thinking continues, as we explore the elements of strategic minds and their significance in shaping visionary and impactful leaders.

1.3 Self-Awareness: The Foundation of Leadership Thinking

Leadership thinking begins with self-awareness. In this section, we emphasize the significance of understanding one's strengths, weaknesses, values, and motivations. We delve into the role of emotional intelligence in leadership and its impact on interpersonal relationships.

Self-awareness, the profound understanding of one's own thoughts, emotions, strengths, and limitations, forms the bedrock of effective leadership thinking. In this section, we explore the significance of self-awareness as the cornerstone of leadership development and its role in shaping visionary, empathetic, and strategic leaders.

1. The Power of Self-Reflection

Leadership thinking begins with introspection and self-reflection. Self-aware leaders take the time to examine their beliefs, values, and motivations. They gain insights into their leadership style and how their actions impact others. Through self-reflection, leaders cultivate a deeper understanding of themselves, setting the stage for personal growth and authentic leadership.

2. Recognizing Strengths and Weaknesses

Self-awareness enables leaders to identify their unique strengths and weaknesses. By acknowledging their areas of expertise and where they may need support, leaders can build complementary teams that compensate for their limitations. Embracing vulnerability and seeking feedback, self-aware leaders continually improve their skills and enhance their leadership effectiveness.

3. Emotional Intelligence and Self-Awareness

Emotional intelligence is closely intertwined with self-awareness. Leaders who understand their emotions and how they influence their decision-making can better regulate their responses to challenging situations. They exhibit emotional resilience, navigating stress and pressure with composure, and fostering a positive work environment for their teams.

4. Authentic Leadership

Authenticity stems from self-awareness. Leaders who are true to themselves, aligning their actions with their values, build trust and credibility with their followers. Authentic leaders engender loyalty and commitment, as their transparency and integrity inspire others to do the same.

5. Mindfulness and Present-Moment Awareness

Practicing mindfulness enhances self-awareness. Mindful leaders cultivate present-moment awareness, allowing them to fully engage in their interactions and decision-making processes. By staying attuned to the needs and emotions of others, mindful leaders build stronger connections with their teams and make more empathetic and insightful choices.

6. Leveraging Self-Awareness for Growth

Self-awareness is not static; it serves as a catalyst for personal growth and leadership development. Leaders who embrace self-awareness as a continuous journey foster a growth mindset, constantly seeking opportunities for learning, improvement, and self-mastery.

7. Impact on Organizational Culture

Leadership thinking permeates an organization's culture, and self-aware leaders play a pivotal role in shaping this culture. Self-awareness encourages open communication, trust, and accountability among team members. In turn, an organization's culture becomes one that values diversity of thought, innovation, and mutual respect.

Conclusion

Self-awareness serves as the bedrock of leadership thinking, enabling leaders to cultivate authenticity, emotional intelligence, and empathy. Leaders who embark on a journey of self-discovery lay the foundation for personal growth and enhanced leadership effectiveness. As we progress in our exploration of leadership thinking, let us recognize self-awareness as a fundamental tool for nurturing visionary and impactful leaders. Embracing self-awareness, we embark on a transformative leadership journey that inspires positive change in both ourselves and those we lead.

1.4 Emotional Intelligence in Leadership

Emotional intelligence is a critical aspect of leadership thinking. We explore the five components of emotional intelligence – self-awareness, self-regulation, motivation, empathy, and social skills – and how they enable leaders to connect with their teams on a deeper level.

Emotional intelligence (EI) is a critical aspect of leadership thinking, encompassing the ability to understand and manage emotions, both in oneself and others. In this section, we delve into the significance of emotional intelligence in effective leadership and explore how leaders with high EI can create a positive and inspiring work environment.

1. The Components of Emotional Intelligence

Emotional intelligence comprises several components that contribute to a leader's overall effectiveness:

a. Self-Awareness: Leaders with self-awareness recognize their emotions and understand how they influence their behaviors and decisions. This self-understanding enables leaders to project authenticity and respond more effectively to challenges.

b. Self-Regulation: Effective leaders possess self-regulation, which allows them to manage their emotions and impulses, even in high-stress situations. They maintain composure, make thoughtful decisions, and prevent emotional reactions from clouding their judgment.

c. Motivation: Motivated leaders exhibit a passion for their work and inspire enthusiasm in their teams. Their intrinsic drive fuels perseverance, setting an example that encourages dedication and commitment from others.

d. Empathy: Empathetic leaders tune into the emotions and perspectives of their team members, fostering deeper connections and trust. They understand the needs of others and respond with compassion and understanding.

e. Social Skills: **Leaders** with strong social skills excel in communication, conflict resolution, and relationship-building. They are adept at inspiring and influencing others, creating a collaborative and supportive work environment.

2. The Impact of Emotional Intelligence on Leadership
Leaders with high emotional intelligence have a profound impact on their teams and organizations:

a. Building Trust and Engagement: **Leaders** who exhibit empathy and understanding build trust and psychological safety within their teams. Employees feel valued and supported, leading to higher engagement and job satisfaction.

b. Effective Communication: **Emotionally** intelligent leaders excel in communication, listening actively and responding with empathy. This open and supportive communication style enhances teamwork and reduces misunderstandings.

c. Conflict Resolution: **Leaders** with emotional intelligence handle conflicts with sensitivity and fairness. They navigate disagreements in a constructive manner, fostering a culture of open dialogue and resolution.

d. Adaptive Leadership: **Emotional** intelligence enables leaders to adapt their leadership style to suit the needs and emotions of their team members. This adaptability enhances the leader's effectiveness in different situations and with diverse individuals.

e. Inspiring Organizational Culture: **Emotionally** intelligent leaders shape a positive organizational culture, one that celebrates diversity, encourages collaboration, and values emotional well-being.

3. Developing Emotional Intelligence

Emotional intelligence is a skill that can be developed and enhanced over time:

a. Self-Reflection and Feedback: **Leaders** can cultivate emotional intelligence through self-reflection and seeking feedback from others. Understanding one's emotional responses and actively seeking input from team members enables leaders to improve their emotional intelligence.

b. Mindfulness Practices: **Mindfulness** practices, such as meditation and mindfulness exercises, can enhance emotional awareness and regulation. Leaders who practice mindfulness develop a greater sense of present-moment awareness and emotional balance.

c. Emotional Intelligence Training: **Organizations** can offer emotional intelligence training to leaders, providing them with the tools and strategies to enhance their emotional intelligence skills and leadership effectiveness.

Conclusion

Emotional intelligence is a fundamental aspect of leadership thinking, enabling leaders to connect with others, build trust, and create a positive work environment. Leaders who develop their emotional intelligence skills foster authentic relationships, inspire engagement, and cultivate a culture of empathy and collaboration. As we continue our exploration of leadership thinking, let us recognize emotional intelligence as a key element in the arsenal of visionary and impactful leaders. By nurturing emotional intelligence, leaders can enrich their own lives and empower those they lead to achieve remarkable success.

1.5 Empathy and Effective Leadership

Empathy is a hallmark of great leaders. In this section, we discuss how empathy fosters trust, enhances communication, and drives team collaboration. We examine real-life examples of leaders who exemplify empathy and its profound impact on organizational culture.

Empathy, the capacity to understand and share the feelings and perspectives of others, is a cornerstone of effective leadership thinking. In this section, we explore the profound significance of empathy in leadership and how empathetic leaders create a positive and inclusive work environment that fosters trust, collaboration, and high performance.

1. The Essence of Empathy in Leadership

Empathy in leadership extends beyond merely sympathizing with others; it involves actively stepping into their shoes to comprehend their emotions, concerns, and motivations. Empathetic leaders exhibit genuine care and consideration for their team members, valuing their contributions and recognizing their individual needs.

2. Building Trust and Psychological Safety

Empathy is the foundation of trust and psychological safety within a team. When employees feel that their leader truly understands and supports them, they are more likely to open up, express their ideas, and take risks. Psychological safety encourages creativity, innovation, and constructive feedback, leading to improved team dynamics and collaboration.

3. Strengthening Relationships and Communication

Empathetic leaders excel in building meaningful relationships with their team members. They actively listen to their concerns, demonstrate understanding, and offer support. This empathetic communication fosters a sense of belonging and loyalty, as employees feel valued and appreciated.

4. Resolving Conflicts and Challenges

Empathetic leaders approach conflicts and challenges with sensitivity and fairness. They consider the perspectives of all parties involved and seek solutions that address everyone's needs. By understanding the emotions underlying conflicts, empathetic leaders can navigate disagreements with compassion and respect.

5. Inspiring Engagement and Motivation

Empathy fuels employee engagement and motivation. When leaders genuinely care about the well-being and growth of their team members, employees are more committed to their work and the organization's mission. Empathetic leaders inspire individuals to go above and beyond, driven by a sense of purpose and fulfillment.

6. Creating a Positive Organizational Culture

An empathetic leader shapes the organizational culture, infusing it with compassion and inclusivity. When empathy is valued and practiced at all levels of the organization, it becomes a guiding principle that permeates the work environment. A culture of empathy promotes diversity, encourages teamwork, and enhances the overall well-being of employees.

7. Emotional Intelligence and Empathy

Empathy and emotional intelligence are closely intertwined. Leaders with high emotional intelligence are better equipped to understand and respond to the emotions of others. They exhibit self-awareness and self-regulation, which enable them to empathize with their team members effectively.

8. Developing Empathy as a Leadership Skill

Empathy is a skill that can be developed and refined:

a. Active Listening: **Leaders** can improve their empathy by actively listening to their team members. Practicing attentive listening and withholding judgment creates a safe space for employees to share their thoughts and feelings.

b. Perspective-Taking: **Leaders** can engage in perspective-taking exercises to understand the experiences and viewpoints of others better. This exercise enhances empathy and broadens their understanding of diverse perspectives.

c. Practicing Empathetic Responses: **Responding with empathy, understanding, and support when team members express their emotions fosters a culture of empathy and emotional well-being.**

Conclusion

Empathy is a transformative quality in leadership thinking, enabling leaders to build trust, strengthen relationships, and create a positive work culture. Empathetic leaders have the power to inspire their teams, encourage collaboration, and drive exceptional performance. As we continue our exploration of leadership thinking, let us recognize empathy as a key element in nurturing visionary and impactful leaders. By embracing empathy, leaders cultivate an environment where individuals thrive and organizations flourish.

1.6 Cognitive Flexibility and Creativity

Leadership thinking is not confined to a rigid framework; it thrives on cognitive flexibility and creativity. We delve into how strategic leaders embrace diverse perspectives, challenge conventional wisdom, and foster a culture of innovation within their organizations.

Cognitive flexibility and creativity are essential components of leadership thinking, empowering leaders to navigate complexity, adapt to change, and foster innovation. In this section, we explore the significance of cognitive flexibility and creativity in effective leadership and how visionary leaders leverage these traits to drive organizational success.

1. Cognitive Flexibility: Embracing Change and Complexity

Cognitive flexibility is the ability to adapt one's thinking and approach in response to new information or shifting circumstances. Effective leaders with cognitive flexibility can view challenges from multiple perspectives, consider diverse solutions, and make well-informed decisions even in dynamic environments.

2. Embracing Change and Uncertainty

In today's rapidly changing world, leaders must embrace change and uncertainty with resilience and an open mindset. Cognitive flexibility allows leaders to see change as an opportunity for growth, rather than a threat, and adapt their strategies to leverage new possibilities.

3. Problem-Solving and Decision-Making

Leaders with cognitive flexibility excel in problem-solving and decision-making. They explore alternative solutions, consider potential consequences, and weigh various factors before arriving at well-considered decisions. This approach enhances their ability to handle complex challenges effectively.

4. Agility and Adaptability

Agility and adaptability are hallmarks of cognitive flexibility. Leaders who can adjust their plans and strategies swiftly in response to new information or unexpected events can navigate uncertainties with ease and lead their teams through transitions.

5. Creativity: Fostering Innovation

Creativity is the ability to generate original and innovative ideas. Visionary leaders harness creativity to inspire their teams and drive innovation within their organizations. They encourage a culture that values creativity, where team members feel empowered to think outside the box and explore novel approaches.

6. Encouraging Risk-Taking and Experimentation

Leaders who prioritize creativity encourage risk-taking and experimentation. They create a safe environment where failure is seen as an opportunity for learning and growth, rather than a reason for punishment. This fosters a culture of innovation and continuous improvement.

7. Leveraging Diversity of Thought

Creativity thrives in diverse environments. Leaders who recognize the value of diverse perspectives and encourage inclusivity can leverage the wealth of ideas that come from different backgrounds and experiences.

8. Nurturing Creativity in Leadership

Leaders can nurture cognitive flexibility and creativity through various practices:

a. Continuous Learning: **Encouraging a culture of continuous learning and curiosity empowers leaders and their teams to stay open to new ideas and perspectives.**

b. Encouraging Idea-Sharing: **Leaders can create platforms for idea-sharing and brainstorming sessions, where team members can contribute and build on each other's ideas.**

c. Recognition and Reward: **Recognizing and rewarding creativity and innovation reinforces their importance within the organization and motivates individuals to continue exploring creative solutions.**

Conclusion

Cognitive flexibility and creativity are indispensable traits in leadership thinking. Leaders who possess these qualities can navigate uncertainty, drive innovation, and inspire their teams to achieve remarkable outcomes. As we continue our exploration of leadership thinking, let us recognize the significance of cognitive flexibility and creativity in nurturing visionary and impactful leaders. By embracing these traits, leaders can lead their organizations to new heights of success and resilience in an ever-changing world.

1.7 Decision-Making in Leadership

At the heart of leadership thinking lies the ability to make well-informed decisions. We explore the decision-making processes that leaders employ, examining the delicate balance between intuition, data-driven insights, and the consideration of potential consequences.

Decision-making is a core aspect of leadership thinking, where leaders face numerous choices that shape the trajectory of their teams and organizations. In this section, we explore the significance of effective decision-making in leadership and how strategic leaders employ various approaches to make informed and impactful choices.

1. The Complexity of Decision-Making in Leadership

Leadership decisions are rarely straightforward; they often involve intricate considerations, trade-offs, and uncertainties. Leaders must grapple with various factors, including available resources, organizational goals, potential risks, and the impact on stakeholders.

2. Data-Driven Decision-Making

Data-driven decision-making is a hallmark of effective leadership thinking. Leaders gather and analyze relevant data, allowing them to make objective assessments and reduce biases. Relying on data empowers leaders to make informed choices that align with organizational objectives.

3. Intuition and Gut Feelings

While data is crucial, leaders also rely on intuition and gut feelings when faced with complex decisions. Intuition is honed through experience and expertise, providing leaders with valuable insights that may not be immediately evident through data analysis.

4. Balancing Speed and Deliberation

Effective leaders strike a balance between making timely decisions and giving matters due deliberation. Some situations demand quick responses, while others require thoughtful analysis. Leaders must gauge the urgency and impact of each decision to determine the appropriate level of speed and consideration.

5. Inclusivity and Collaboration

Inclusive decision-making involves soliciting input from various stakeholders and team members. By involving relevant parties in the decision-making process, leaders benefit from diverse perspectives and foster a sense of ownership and commitment to the chosen course of action.

6. The Role of Risk Assessment

Leaders assess risks associated with different decisions and develop strategies to mitigate potential negative consequences. They weigh risks against potential rewards, making decisions that strike a balance between innovation and prudence.

7. Decision-Making Under Uncertainty

Leaders often face uncertainty and ambiguity, making decision-making more challenging. In such situations, leaders must be adaptable, agile, and ready to adjust their strategies as new information becomes available.

8. Embracing Accountability

Leaders take responsibility for their decisions, whether they lead to success or failure. Embracing accountability fosters trust within the team and encourages a culture of learning from experiences, which drives continuous improvement.

9. Ethical Decision-Making

Ethics is an integral aspect of leadership thinking. Leaders must consider ethical implications and the impact of their decisions on various stakeholders. Ethical decision-making builds trust, credibility, and sustainable relationships within and outside the organization.

10. Learning from Mistakes

Leaders who acknowledge and learn from their mistakes create a culture that encourages innovation and growth. Rather than avoiding failures, leaders view them as opportunities for improvement and adjust their decision-making processes accordingly.

Conclusion

Decision-making is a fundamental element of leadership thinking, influencing the success and direction of organizations. Effective leaders employ a combination of data analysis, intuition, collaboration, and ethical considerations to make informed and impactful choices. As we continue our exploration of leadership thinking, let us recognize the significance of decision-making in nurturing visionary and impactful leaders. By mastering the art of decision-making, leaders can lead their teams through challenges and opportunities, steering their organizations towards sustainable growth and success.

1.8 Ethical Considerations

Ethics is an integral aspect of leadership thinking. In this section, we highlight the importance of ethical decision-making, integrity, and transparency in leadership roles. We explore the ethical dilemmas leaders face and the moral compass that guides their actions.

Ethical considerations form an integral part of leadership thinking, shaping how leaders make decisions, interact with others, and guide their organizations. In this section, we explore the profound significance of ethics in effective leadership and how ethical leaders foster trust, integrity, and sustainable success.

1. Defining Ethical Leadership

Ethical leadership involves making decisions and taking actions that align with moral principles and values. Ethical leaders prioritize honesty, fairness, transparency, and accountability in their interactions and decision-making processes.

2. The Impact of Ethical Leadership

Ethical leadership has far-reaching effects on individuals, teams, and organizations:

a. Building Trust and Credibility: Ethical leaders earn the trust and respect of their team members and stakeholders. Trust is the foundation of strong relationships, fostering a collaborative and cohesive work environment.

b. Organizational Reputation: **Ethical leadership enhances the reputation of an organization, attracting top talent, customers, and business partners who value integrity.**

c. Employee Engagement and Loyalty: **Ethical leaders prioritize the well-being of their employees, leading to higher levels of engagement, job satisfaction, and loyalty.**

d. Sustainability and Longevity: **Ethical leadership contributes to the long-term sustainability and success of an organization. By making decisions that consider the interests of all stakeholders, ethical leaders build a strong foundation for enduring growth.**

3. Ethical Decision-Making

Ethical decision-making involves evaluating the moral implications of choices and their potential impact on various stakeholders. Ethical leaders consider not only legal and financial consequences but also the ethical dimension of their decisions.

4. Integrity and Leading by Example

Integrity is a core value of ethical leadership. Leaders who demonstrate integrity lead by example, exhibiting consistency between their words and actions. This consistency inspires their teams to act ethically and uphold the organization's values.

5. Ethical Dilemmas and Complexities

Ethical leadership often involves grappling with ethical dilemmas and complexities. Leaders must navigate situations where ethical values may clash, requiring thoughtful analysis and consideration of potential consequences.

6. Transparency and Open Communication

Ethical leaders prioritize transparency in their communication. Openness and honesty create an environment where team members feel comfortable expressing their concerns and contributing to decision-making.

7. Embracing Diversity and Inclusivity

Ethical leadership embraces diversity and inclusivity. Leaders value diverse perspectives, treat everyone with respect, and ensure equal opportunities for all team members.

8. Cultivating an Ethical Organizational Culture

Ethical leaders shape the organizational culture to foster ethical behavior. They establish clear ethical guidelines and policies, encouraging employees to uphold ethical standards in their daily actions.

Conclusion

Ethical considerations are at the core of leadership thinking, influencing the culture, decision-making, and success of organizations. Ethical leaders prioritize integrity, transparency, and inclusivity, building trust and credibility with their teams and stakeholders. As we continue our exploration of leadership thinking, let us recognize the significance of ethical considerations in nurturing visionary and impactful leaders. By exemplifying ethical leadership, leaders can create a positive and sustainable impact, making a difference in the lives of their team members and the success of their organizations.

1.9 Leadership Thinking in Diverse Contexts

Leadership thinking is not one-size-fits-all; it adapts to diverse contexts and challenges. We examine how leadership thinking varies across different industries, cultures, and organizational structures, emphasizing the need for flexible and adaptable leadership approaches.

Leadership thinking is not a one-size-fits-all approach; it adapts and evolves in diverse contexts and environments. In this section, we explore the dynamic nature of leadership thinking and how visionary leaders adjust their strategies to effectively lead in different industries, cultures, and organizational structures.

1. Industry-Specific Leadership Thinking

Leadership thinking varies across industries, each with its unique challenges and opportunities:

a. Technology and Innovation: Leaders in technology-driven industries must embrace rapid change, foster innovation, and adapt to disruptive technologies. They prioritize agility and forward-thinking to maintain a competitive edge.

b. Healthcare and Wellness: Leaders in healthcare focus on patient care and well-being. They demonstrate empathy and ethical decision-making while navigating complex regulatory landscapes.

c. Finance and Banking: Leaders in finance prioritize risk management, compliance, and financial stability. They make data-driven decisions and maintain transparency to build trust with customers and investors.

d. Education and Academia: Leaders in education foster a culture of learning and growth. They empower educators, students, and administrators to achieve academic excellence.

2. Cross-Cultural Leadership Thinking

Effective cross-cultural leadership thinking recognizes and respects cultural differences:

a. Communication: Cross-cultural leaders adapt their communication styles to ensure clarity and avoid misunderstandings. They are sensitive to non-verbal cues and diverse communication norms.

b. Values and Norms: Leaders understand and appreciate the values and norms of different cultures, incorporating cultural diversity into their organizational practices.

c. Inclusivity: Cross-cultural leaders create inclusive environments, embracing diversity of thought and experiences. They promote cultural understanding and collaboration within diverse teams.

d. Global Perspective: Leaders with a global perspective understand the interconnectedness of economies and cultures, making decisions that consider the broader impact.

3. Leadership in Different Organizational Structures

Leadership thinking adapts to the structure and size of an organization:

a. Small Businesses and Startups: Leaders in small businesses and startups wear multiple hats and prioritize agility, innovation, and growth.

b. Large Corporations: Leaders in large corporations focus on managing complex hierarchies, driving organizational alignment, and ensuring operational efficiency.

c. Nonprofit Organizations: Leaders in nonprofits prioritize their mission and impact. They demonstrate empathy and transparency in their efforts to address societal needs.

d. Government and Public Sector: Leaders in the public sector navigate bureaucracy and accountability. They work towards serving the public interest and making evidence-based decisions.

Conclusion

Leadership thinking is adaptable and multifaceted, reflecting the diverse contexts in which leaders operate. Visionary leaders recognize that effective leadership requires an understanding of industry-specific challenges, cultural nuances, and organizational structures. By embracing diversity and adjusting their strategies accordingly, leaders can inspire and motivate their teams, driving success and making a positive impact in their unique environments. As we continue our exploration of leadership thinking, let us recognize the value of adaptability and cultural competence in nurturing visionary and impactful leaders across diverse contexts.

Chapter 2: The Elements of Strategic Minds

Strategic minds are characterized by their ability to think critically, envision the future, and devise effective plans to achieve long-term objectives. In this chapter, we explore the key elements that define strategic minds and how these attributes contribute to visionary and impactful leadership.

1. Visionary Thinking

Strategic minds possess a visionary outlook, imagining possibilities beyond the status quo. They articulate a compelling vision that inspires others, aligning teams toward a common purpose and motivating them to pursue ambitious goals.

Visionary thinking is a foundational element of strategic minds, empowering leaders to imagine a compelling future and inspire others to work towards that shared vision. In this chapter, we delve into the significance of visionary thinking in leadership and how it drives organizational success.

1. Defining Visionary Thinking

Visionary thinking involves the ability to envision a future that goes beyond the current state. It is a forward-looking perspective that transcends immediate challenges and focuses on long-term goals and possibilities.

2. Articulating a Compelling Vision

Visionary leaders articulate a compelling vision that resonates with their teams and stakeholders. This vision serves as a guiding star, providing a clear sense of purpose and direction.

3. Aligning Teams towards a Common Purpose

A visionary leader's ability to communicate their vision aligns teams towards a common purpose. When team members understand and embrace the collective goal, they become more motivated, engaged, and committed to achieving it.

4. Inspiring Innovation and Creativity

Visionary thinking sparks innovation and creativity within the organization. A compelling vision encourages individuals to think beyond traditional boundaries, explore new possibilities, and devise inventive solutions.

5. Navigating Complexity

In a rapidly changing world, visionary thinking helps leaders navigate complexity and uncertainty. By envisioning potential challenges and opportunities, leaders can proactively shape strategies to address them.

6. Building Resilience

Visionary thinking fosters resilience within an organization. In the face of setbacks, a clear vision helps teams stay focused on the bigger picture, overcome obstacles, and adapt to changing circumstances.

7. Attracting and Retaining Talent

A powerful vision attracts and retains top talent. Individuals seek to be part of a purpose-driven organization, where they can contribute to a meaningful mission and make a positive impact.

8. Balancing Ambition and Realism

Visionary thinking requires a balance between ambition and realism. Leaders must set ambitious yet achievable goals, inspiring their teams to stretch their capabilities while ensuring their efforts remain grounded in practicality.

9. Continual Progression

Visionary thinking involves continual progression towards the vision. Leaders regularly assess progress, adjust strategies as needed, and celebrate milestones to maintain momentum and enthusiasm.

10. Influencing Organizational Culture

Visionary leaders shape the organizational culture through their vision. A culture aligned with the vision fosters shared values, a sense of belonging, and a collective commitment to success.

Conclusion

Visionary thinking is a cornerstone of strategic minds, propelling leaders and organizations towards greatness. Leaders who embrace visionary thinking envision a future of possibility and purpose, inspiring their teams to strive for excellence and embrace innovation. As we conclude our exploration of visionary thinking, let us recognize that visionary leaders have the power to shape the trajectory of their organizations and make a transformative impact on the world. By fostering visionary thinking, leaders can ignite a sense of purpose, ignite a passion for progress, and drive exceptional results that leave a lasting legacy.

2. Analytical and Critical Thinking

Analytical and critical thinking are essential elements of strategic minds. Leaders with these attributes gather and analyze data, identify patterns, and draw insights that inform their decision-making. They weigh pros and cons, consider various scenarios, and make well-informed choices.

Analytical and critical thinking are vital elements of strategic minds, enabling leaders to make well-informed decisions, solve complex problems, and navigate uncertainties with confidence. In this chapter, we explore the significance of analytical and critical thinking in leadership and how these cognitive skills drive organizational success.

1. Defining Analytical and Critical Thinking

Analytical thinking involves breaking down complex problems into smaller components and examining them systematically. Critical thinking, on the other hand, entails evaluating information objectively, identifying assumptions, and drawing reasoned conclusions.

2. Data-Driven Decision Making

Leaders with analytical thinking skills rely on data to make informed decisions. They gather relevant information, analyze trends, and use data insights to assess potential risks and rewards.

3. Identifying Opportunities and Risks

Analytical thinking helps leaders identify opportunities and risks. By analyzing market trends, competitor behavior, and industry developments, leaders can capitalize on emerging opportunities and proactively address potential challenges.

4. Evaluating Alternatives

Critical thinking empowers leaders to evaluate various alternatives and consider the consequences of each option. This evaluation process ensures decisions are well-rounded and take into account multiple perspectives.

5. Problem-Solving and Root Cause Analysis

Analytical and critical thinking go hand in hand in problem-solving. Leaders use these skills to identify the root causes of challenges, enabling them to devise effective solutions that address underlying issues.

6. Strategic Planning and Forecasting

Strategic minds rely on analytical thinking in strategic planning. They analyze data, market trends, and consumer behavior to forecast future scenarios and develop proactive strategies.

7. Informed Risk Management

Critical thinking helps leaders assess risks objectively and consider the probability and potential impact of each risk. This informed risk management approach allows leaders to make calculated decisions that balance innovation with prudence.

8. Continuous Learning and Adaptability

Analytical and critical thinking foster a culture of continuous learning and adaptability. Leaders with these skills seek feedback, learn from past experiences, and adjust strategies based on new information.

9. Balancing Intuition and Evidence

Strategic minds balance intuition and evidence-based decision-making. While intuition provides valuable insights, leaders validate their hunches with data and critical analysis.

10. Promoting a Culture of Evidence-Based Thinking

Leaders with analytical and critical thinking skills promote a culture of evidence-based thinking within their organizations. They encourage team members to approach problems thoughtfully and make decisions supported by data and evidence.

Conclusion

Analytical and critical thinking are indispensable traits of strategic minds, empowering leaders to navigate complex challenges and seize opportunities with clarity and confidence. Leaders who embrace these cognitive skills make data-driven decisions, foster a culture of continuous improvement, and promote evidence-based thinking throughout their organizations. As we conclude our exploration of analytical and critical thinking, let us recognize that these skills are not only essential in problem-solving but also in driving innovation, adaptability, and long-term success. By cultivating analytical and critical thinking, leaders can elevate their decision-making, inspire their teams, and create a culture of strategic excellence.

3. Long-Term Orientation

Strategic minds have a long-term orientation, focusing on sustainable success rather than short-term gains. They create strategies that consider future challenges and opportunities, positioning their organizations for continued growth and relevance.

Long-term orientation is a fundamental element of strategic minds, guiding leaders to focus on sustainable success and enduring impact. In this chapter, we explore the significance of long-term orientation in leadership and how it shapes strategic thinking and decision-making.

1. Defining Long-Term Orientation

Long-term orientation involves a perspective that extends beyond immediate results and seeks to create lasting value. Leaders with long-term orientation prioritize the future success and growth of their organizations over short-term gains.

2. Strategic Planning and Goal Setting

Leaders with long-term orientation engage in strategic planning and goal setting that align with the organization's vision and values. They set ambitious yet achievable objectives that drive progress over time.

3. Building Resilience

Long-term orientation fosters resilience within an organization. Leaders anticipate potential challenges and invest in building a strong foundation to weather unforeseen circumstances.

4. Balancing Short-Term and Long-Term Priorities

Strategic minds strike a balance between short-term and long-term priorities. While they address immediate needs, they never lose sight of the organization's overarching vision and strategic objectives.

5. Continuous Improvement

Leaders with long-term orientation foster a culture of continuous improvement. They seek feedback, analyze performance metrics, and implement iterative changes to enhance efficiency and effectiveness.

6. Investment in Human Capital

Long-term orientation emphasizes investment in human capital. Leaders recognize that nurturing and developing their employees leads to a more skilled, engaged, and loyal workforce.

7. Innovation and Adaptation

Strategic minds embrace innovation and adaptation to stay relevant in a dynamic world. They invest in research and development and continuously explore new opportunities for growth.

8. Stakeholder Management

Leaders with long-term orientation prioritize stakeholder management. They consider the interests of various stakeholders, including employees, customers, investors, and the community, to build sustainable relationships.

9. Corporate Social Responsibility

Long-term orientation includes a commitment to corporate social responsibility. Leaders acknowledge their impact on society and take proactive steps to contribute positively to the communities they serve.

10. Legacy and Impact

Leaders with long-term orientation aspire to leave a lasting legacy and make a positive impact on their organizations and the world. They view their leadership as part of a broader journey of growth and progress.

Conclusion

Long-term orientation is a defining trait of strategic minds, propelling leaders to build enduring success and create a positive impact. Leaders with this perspective prioritize sustainable growth, innovation, and resilience, creating a culture of continuous improvement and strategic excellence. As we conclude our exploration of long-term orientation, let us recognize that leaders who embrace this element are not merely concerned with immediate results; they are architects of a brighter and more visionary future. By adopting a long-term orientation, leaders can inspire their teams, fortify their organizations against uncertainties, and achieve remarkable and enduring success.

4. Adaptability and Flexibility

Adaptability and flexibility are hallmark traits of strategic minds. These leaders anticipate changes in the dynamic business landscape and respond proactively, adjusting strategies as needed to maintain a competitive advantage.

Adaptability and flexibility are key elements of strategic minds, enabling leaders to thrive in dynamic and ever-changing environments. In this chapter, we explore the significance of adaptability and flexibility in leadership and how these traits empower leaders to navigate uncertainties with resilience and ingenuity.

1. Embracing Change

Strategic minds embrace change as an opportunity for growth rather than a hindrance. Leaders with adaptability and flexibility understand that change is inevitable and actively seek ways to respond proactively to new circumstances.

2. Agility in Decision-Making

Adaptable leaders demonstrate agility in decision-making. They can pivot swiftly, adjust strategies, and make course corrections based on emerging information or changing market conditions.

3. Resilience in Adversity

Leaders with adaptability and flexibility exhibit resilience in the face of adversity. They remain composed during challenging times, learn from setbacks, and inspire their teams to persevere.

4. Openness to New Ideas

Adaptable and flexible leaders maintain an open mind to new ideas and diverse perspectives. They encourage creativity and innovation, valuing input from their team members and stakeholders.

5. Learning Orientation

Strategic minds have a learning orientation, continuously seeking opportunities to acquire new knowledge and skills. They recognize that learning is a lifelong journey that fuels growth and adaptation.

6. Multi-Dimensional Thinking

Adaptable leaders engage in multi-dimensional thinking, considering various scenarios and potential outcomes. They anticipate challenges and devise contingency plans to address uncertainties.

7. Navigating Ambiguity

Leaders with adaptability and flexibility navigate ambiguity with poise. They resist the urge to make hasty decisions based on incomplete information and instead seek clarity through thoughtful analysis.

8. Embracing Innovation

Adaptability and flexibility foster a culture of innovation within an organization. Leaders encourage experimentation and support creative solutions to stay ahead in a competitive landscape.

9. Collaborative Approach

Adaptable leaders promote a collaborative approach. They encourage open communication, inviting feedback and contributions from team members to enhance adaptability.

10. Leading by Example

Above all, adaptable and flexible leaders lead by example. They embody the traits they seek in their teams, demonstrating resilience, agility, and a positive attitude in the face of change.

Conclusion

Adaptability and flexibility are indispensable traits of strategic minds, empowering leaders to thrive in an ever-evolving world. Leaders who embrace these traits are better equipped to navigate uncertainties, seize opportunities, and inspire their teams to embrace change with confidence. As we conclude our exploration of adaptability and flexibility, let us recognize that these traits are not only essential in leadership but also in driving innovation and creating a dynamic and resilient organizational culture. By cultivating adaptability and flexibility, leaders can elevate their thinking, foster a culture of creativity and continuous improvement, and achieve exceptional results in the face of complexity and change.

5. Risk Management

Strategic minds engage in prudent risk management. They assess potential risks and rewards, making calculated decisions that embrace innovation while mitigating potential negative outcomes.

Risk management is a critical element of strategic minds, allowing leaders to make calculated decisions that balance innovation with prudence. In this chapter, we explore the significance of risk management in leadership and how strategic leaders navigate uncertainties with foresight and responsibility.

1. Identifying Risks

Strategic leaders identify potential risks by conducting thorough assessments of internal and external factors. They analyze market trends, competitor behavior, and other variables to anticipate challenges that may impact the organization's objectives.

2. Assessing Risk Impact and Probability

Leaders with strong risk management skills assess the impact and probability of identified risks. This evaluation allows them to prioritize risks based on their potential consequences and likelihood of occurrence.

3. Making Informed Decisions

Risk management enables leaders to make informed decisions that consider potential risks and rewards. Leaders weigh the potential benefits of an opportunity against the associated risks before proceeding.

4. Mitigating Risks

Strategic minds actively work to mitigate identified risks. They develop contingency plans and implement measures to reduce the impact of potential adverse events.

5. Balancing Innovation and Prudence

Effective risk management involves striking a balance between innovation and prudence. Strategic leaders encourage innovation while ensuring that risks are taken in a responsible and controlled manner.

6. Learning from Past Experiences

Leaders with strong risk management skills learn from past experiences and apply these lessons to future decision-making. Analyzing previous successes and failures helps them refine their risk management approach.

7. Embracing Ethical Risk Management

Ethical considerations are integral to risk management. Leaders assess risks not only from a financial perspective but also from an ethical standpoint, ensuring decisions align with the organization's values.

8. Creating a Risk-Aware Culture

Strategic leaders foster a risk-aware culture within their organizations. They encourage employees to report potential risks and promote open communication regarding risk-related matters.

9. Proactive Risk Management

Strategic minds engage in proactive risk management rather than reacting to crises. By anticipating and addressing risks in advance, leaders minimize the likelihood and impact of negative outcomes.

10. Continual Evaluation and Improvement

Risk management is an ongoing process. Strategic leaders continually evaluate the effectiveness of their risk management strategies and make improvements as needed.

Conclusion

Risk management is a fundamental element of strategic minds, guiding leaders to make responsible decisions that drive sustainable success. Leaders who prioritize risk management skills anticipate challenges, seize opportunities, and safeguard the organization against potential adversities. As we conclude our exploration of risk management, let us recognize that effective risk management requires a forward-thinking approach that considers both the potential benefits and consequences of decisions. By cultivating strong risk management skills, leaders can navigate uncertainties with foresight and responsibility, fostering resilience and achieving remarkable results in an ever-changing world.

6. Innovative Problem-Solving

Strategic minds foster a culture of innovative problem-solving. They encourage creativity, out-of-the-box thinking, and experimentation to address complex challenges and capitalize on emerging opportunities.

Innovative problem-solving is a hallmark of strategic minds, enabling leaders to address complex challenges with creativity and ingenuity. In this chapter, we explore the significance of innovative problem-solving in leadership and how it drives organizational growth and success.

1. Defining Innovative Problem-Solving

Innovative problem-solving involves thinking outside the box to devise original and creative solutions to complex issues. Strategic leaders encourage their teams to explore unconventional approaches and challenge conventional thinking.

2. Encouraging Creativity

Leaders with innovative problem-solving skills foster a culture of creativity within their organizations. They encourage brainstorming, idea-sharing, and experimentation to generate innovative solutions.

3. Embracing Ambiguity

Strategic minds embrace ambiguity and resist the urge to rush into solutions prematurely. They remain patient and open-minded during the problem-solving process, allowing space for innovative ideas to emerge.

4. Collaboration and Diverse Perspectives

Innovative problem-solving often benefits from collaboration and diverse perspectives. Leaders facilitate cross-functional teamwork, valuing contributions from individuals with different backgrounds and expertise.

5. Experimentation and Risk-Taking

Leaders with innovative problem-solving skills encourage experimentation and risk-taking. They view failures as opportunities to learn and adjust strategies accordingly.

6. Human-Centered Approach

Innovative problem-solving incorporates a human-centered approach. Leaders prioritize understanding the needs and desires of stakeholders to create solutions that truly address their concerns.

7. Continuous Improvement and Iteration

Strategic minds view problem-solving as an iterative process. They continuously seek feedback, evaluate the effectiveness of solutions, and refine approaches for ongoing improvement.

8. Incorporating Technology and Data

Leaders leverage technology and data to support innovative problem-solving. They use data analytics and technological tools to gain insights and inform decision-making.

9. Fostering a Culture of Innovation

Innovative problem-solving thrives in a culture of innovation. Strategic leaders create an environment that encourages risk-taking, rewards creativity, and supports continuous learning.

10. Applying Solutions Across Contexts

Innovative problem-solving extends beyond individual challenges. Strategic minds seek solutions that can be applied across different contexts and create a lasting impact.

Conclusion

Innovative problem-solving is a defining characteristic of strategic minds, driving leaders and organizations to navigate complexities with creativity and resourcefulness. Leaders who embrace innovative problem-solving inspire their teams to challenge the status quo, explore new possibilities, and achieve breakthroughs. As we conclude our exploration of innovative problem-solving, let us recognize that it is a mindset that can be cultivated through openness to new ideas, collaboration, and a commitment to continuous improvement. By fostering innovative problem-solving, leaders can unlock their full potential, foster a culture of creativity, and drive exceptional results that set their organizations apart in a dynamic and competitive landscape.

7. Strategic Communication

Effective strategic minds excel in communication. They articulate their vision clearly and engage stakeholders in a compelling dialogue. Their communication skills inspire buy-in and create a shared sense of purpose.

Strategic communication is a critical element of strategic minds, empowering leaders to articulate their vision, build trust, and inspire action. In this chapter, we explore the significance of strategic communication in leadership and how effective communication drives organizational success.

1. Defining Strategic Communication

Strategic communication involves purposeful and intentional messaging to convey information and influence stakeholders. Leaders with strategic communication skills tailor their messages to align with their vision and objectives.

2. Articulating a Compelling Vision

Strategic minds excel in articulating a compelling vision. Through clear and inspiring communication, leaders communicate their long-term goals, motivating their teams to rally behind a shared purpose.

3. Building Trust and Credibility

Effective strategic communication builds trust and credibility. Leaders who communicate openly, honestly, and transparently foster strong relationships with their teams and stakeholders.

4. Adaptability in Communication

Strategic leaders adapt their communication style to suit diverse audiences. They recognize that different stakeholders may require varying levels of detail and respond to tailored approaches.

5. Listening and Feedback

Strategic communication is a two-way process. Leaders actively listen to their teams, seek feedback, and incorporate valuable insights into their decision-making.

6. Inspiring Action

Leaders with strategic communication skills inspire action. Their messages resonate with their audience, driving commitment, and motivating individuals to take initiative.

7. Crisis Communication

Strategic minds excel in crisis communication. During challenging times, leaders communicate with empathy and transparency, providing reassurance and a sense of direction to their teams.

8. Storytelling and Narrative

Leaders leverage storytelling and narrative to make their messages memorable and impactful. Through compelling narratives, they connect with emotions, making complex ideas more relatable.

9. Communicating Company Values

Strategic leaders consistently communicate the organization's values, emphasizing their importance in decision-making and daily operations.

10. Leveraging Communication Channels

Effective strategic communication leverages various communication channels to reach diverse stakeholders. Leaders embrace digital platforms, traditional media, and face-to-face interactions to ensure messages are effectively disseminated.

Conclusion

Strategic communication is a pivotal skill that distinguishes visionary leaders from the rest. Leaders who excel in strategic communication inspire and motivate their teams, earn the trust of stakeholders, and create a culture of open dialogue and collaboration. As we conclude our exploration of strategic communication, let us recognize that it is more than conveying information; it is an art that requires empathy, adaptability, and a deep understanding of the audience. By honing strategic communication skills, leaders can elevate their influence, drive organizational alignment, and achieve remarkable results that leave a lasting impact.

8. Collaboration and Empowerment

Strategic minds value collaboration and empowerment. They seek diverse perspectives, involve key stakeholders in decision-making, and delegate responsibilities to capable team members, fostering a culture of collective ownership.

Collaboration and empowerment are essential elements of strategic minds, fostering a culture of collective ownership and maximizing the potential of teams. In this chapter, we explore the significance of collaboration and empowerment in leadership and how these traits drive innovation and success.

1. Embracing Collaborative Leadership

Strategic leaders embrace collaborative leadership, valuing diverse perspectives and encouraging active participation from their team members. They understand that collective intelligence fuels innovation and problem-solving.

2. Building High-Performing Teams

Leaders who prioritize collaboration build high-performing teams. They create an environment where individuals feel empowered to share ideas, take initiative, and contribute to the organization's success.

3. Promoting Open Communication

Effective collaboration thrives in an environment of open communication. Strategic leaders foster a culture where team members feel comfortable expressing their thoughts, concerns, and feedback.

4. Recognizing and Valuing Contributions

Empowering leaders recognize and value the contributions of their team members. They celebrate achievements, provide constructive feedback, and foster a sense of pride in collective accomplishments.

5. Delegating Authority and Responsibility

Leaders with empowerment skills delegate authority and responsibility to capable team members. This delegation fosters a sense of ownership and accountability, encouraging individuals to excel in their roles.

6. Encouraging Skill Development

Strategic minds encourage skill development and growth within their teams. They provide opportunities for professional development, enabling team members to reach their full potential.

7. Building a Culture of Trust

Collaboration and empowerment are rooted in trust. Leaders who trust their teams to make informed decisions and take ownership create a culture that values autonomy and accountability.

8. Facilitating Cross-Functional Collaboration

Strategic leaders facilitate cross-functional collaboration, breaking down silos and encouraging interdepartmental cooperation. This approach fosters a holistic view of the organization's goals and challenges.

9. Embracing Diversity and Inclusivity

Leaders who prioritize collaboration and empowerment embrace diversity and inclusivity. They value the unique contributions of individuals from different backgrounds and perspectives.

10. Nurturing Emerging Leaders

Empowering leaders invest in nurturing emerging leaders within their organization. They provide mentorship and growth opportunities, ensuring the continuity of strategic thinking and leadership.

Conclusion

Collaboration and empowerment are the cornerstones of strategic minds, unlocking the full potential of teams and driving organizational success. Leaders who prioritize collaboration create an inclusive and innovative culture, where diverse talents come together to solve complex challenges. Empowerment fosters a sense of ownership and accountability, inspiring individuals to take initiative and make a meaningful impact. As we conclude our exploration of collaboration and empowerment, let us recognize that these traits are not only about working together; they are about fostering an environment where every individual feels valued and inspired to contribute their best. By embracing collaboration and empowerment, leaders can nurture a dynamic and engaged workforce, elevate the capabilities of their organization, and achieve remarkable results that set them apart as visionary leaders.

9. Continuous Learning

Strategic minds are lifelong learners, staying abreast of industry trends, technological advancements, and best practices. They cultivate a growth mindset, encouraging themselves and their teams to evolve and adapt.

Continuous learning is a fundamental element of strategic minds, enabling leaders to stay relevant, adapt to changes, and drive innovation within their organizations. In this chapter, we explore the significance of continuous learning in leadership and how it fosters personal growth and organizational success.

1. Embracing Lifelong Learning

Strategic leaders embrace lifelong learning as a cornerstone of their leadership journey. They recognize that knowledge and skills must be continually updated to navigate the complexities of an ever-changing world.

2. Cultivating a Growth Mindset

Leaders with a growth mindset view challenges as opportunities for learning and growth. They encourage their teams to adopt a similar mindset, fostering resilience and a willingness to embrace new challenges.

3. Staying Informed of Industry Trends

Continuous learning involves staying informed of industry trends, technological advancements, and best practices. Leaders leverage this knowledge to make informed decisions and drive innovation.

4. Seeking Feedback and Self-Reflection

Strategic minds actively seek feedback and engage in self-reflection. They use feedback to identify areas for improvement and take proactive steps to enhance their leadership skills.

5. Encouraging a Learning Culture

Leaders who prioritize continuous learning foster a learning culture within their organizations. They encourage employees to pursue professional development and provide resources to support learning initiatives.

6. Learning from Failure

Continuous learning involves learning from failures and setbacks. Strategic leaders view failures as opportunities to identify areas for improvement and drive innovation.

7. Engaging in Professional Development

Leaders with a commitment to continuous learning engage in ongoing professional development. They attend workshops, conferences, and courses to expand their knowledge and skillset.

8. Mentoring and Coaching

Strategic minds engage in mentoring and coaching, both as mentors and mentees. They recognize the value of learning from experienced individuals and supporting the growth of emerging talent.

9. Building a Learning Network

Continuous learning involves building a learning network of peers and industry experts. Leaders leverage their network to share insights, collaborate on challenges, and gain diverse perspectives.

10. Applying Learning to Decision-Making

Leaders who prioritize continuous learning apply their knowledge and insights to decision-making. Informed decisions based on learning experiences drive organizational growth and success.

Conclusion

Continuous learning is a defining trait of strategic minds, empowering leaders to adapt, innovate, and lead with confidence. Leaders who prioritize continuous learning inspire their teams to embrace a growth mindset, fostering a culture of curiosity and exploration. As we conclude our exploration of continuous learning, let us recognize that leaders who commit to lifelong learning elevate their leadership capabilities, drive innovation, and position their organizations for sustained success. By embracing continuous learning, leaders can stay at the forefront of their fields, inspire their teams, and achieve remarkable results that leave a lasting impact on their organizations and beyond.

10. Ethical Leadership

Ethics are central to strategic minds. They prioritize integrity, transparency, and responsible leadership, considering the ethical implications of their decisions.

Ethical leadership is a cornerstone of strategic minds, guiding leaders to make principled decisions and cultivate a culture of integrity within their organizations. In this chapter, we explore the significance of ethical leadership in guiding ethical behavior and driving sustainable success.

1. Defining Ethical Leadership

Ethical leadership involves making decisions guided by moral principles and values. Leaders with ethical leadership prioritize doing what is right, even when faced with difficult choices.

2. Leading by Example

Ethical leaders lead by example, demonstrating integrity, transparency, and ethical conduct in their actions and decisions. Their behavior sets the tone for the organization's ethical culture.

3. Ethical Decision-Making Framework

Strategic minds use an ethical decision-making framework to assess the ethical implications of their choices. They consider the impact on stakeholders, organizational values, and long-term consequences.

4. Prioritizing Stakeholder Welfare

Ethical leaders prioritize the welfare of all stakeholders, including employees, customers, investors, and the community. They seek to create shared value that benefits both the organization and society.

5. Transparency and Open Communication

Ethical leadership involves transparency and open communication. Leaders share information openly, allowing stakeholders to make informed decisions based on accurate and complete information.

6. Compliance and Corporate Governance

Strategic minds uphold compliance with laws and regulations and prioritize strong corporate governance. They establish internal controls and processes to ensure ethical conduct and accountability.

7. Ethical Conflict Resolution

Ethical leaders address ethical conflicts proactively and fairly. They encourage open discussions to resolve ethical dilemmas and maintain a culture of ethical behavior.

8. Consideration of Ethical Implications

Leaders with ethical leadership skills consider the ethical implications of their decisions as part of their overall strategic thinking. They integrate ethical considerations into their long-term planning.

9. Balancing Stakeholder Interests

Ethical leadership involves balancing the interests of different stakeholders to find ethical solutions that create shared value for the organization and society.

10. Sustainable and Responsible Leadership

Strategic minds recognize the responsibility of leadership and strive for sustainable and responsible practices. They aim to leave a positive and lasting impact on the organization and the world.

Conclusion

Ethical leadership is a defining trait of strategic minds, guiding leaders to make principled decisions and foster a culture of integrity within their organizations. Leaders who prioritize ethical leadership inspire trust and respect, creating a strong foundation for sustained success. As we conclude our exploration of ethical leadership, let us recognize that ethical conduct is not merely a moral obligation; it is a strategic imperative that drives long-term value and impacts the reputation and legacy of the organization. By embracing ethical leadership, leaders can elevate their influence, drive a positive organizational culture, and achieve remarkable results that contribute to a better world for all stakeholders.

Chapter 3: Decision-Making Strategies

In Chapter 3, we delve into the decision-making strategies employed by strategic minds. Effective decision-making is crucial for leaders to navigate complexities, seize opportunities, and achieve organizational goals. This chapter explores various decision-making approaches and how strategic leaders use them to make well-informed and impactful choices.

1. Rational Decision Making

Rational decision-making involves a systematic and logical approach to problem-solving. Strategic minds carefully assess available information, evaluate alternatives, and choose the option that best aligns with their vision and objectives.

Rational decision-making is a systematic and logical approach used by strategic minds to make well-informed choices. In this chapter, we explore the significance of rational decision-making in leadership and how it enhances the decision-making process.

1. Defining Rational Decision Making

Rational decision-making involves a structured process of identifying a problem, gathering relevant information, evaluating alternatives, and selecting the best option based on logical reasoning.

2. Identifying the Problem

Strategic leaders begin by identifying the problem or opportunity they need to address. They clarify the objectives and criteria for a successful outcome.

3. Gathering Relevant Information

To make rational decisions, leaders gather relevant information from various sources. They consider data, expert opinions, and market trends to gain a comprehensive understanding of the situation.

4. Analyzing Alternatives

Strategic minds explore multiple alternatives to address the problem. They analyze the potential benefits, risks, and implications of each option to assess its viability.

5. Weighing Pros and Cons

Rational decision-making involves weighing the pros and cons of each alternative. Leaders consider the potential benefits and drawbacks to make an objective evaluation.

6. Considering Constraints and Resources

Strategic leaders consider constraints and available resources during the decision-making process. They align their choices with the organization's capabilities and limitations.

7. Making a Decision

After a thorough analysis, leaders make the best choice based on the available information and their strategic objectives. They commit to the decision with confidence.

8. Implementing the Decision

Rational decision-making does not end with the choice; it extends to the implementation phase. Strategic leaders ensure a well-planned and seamless execution of the decision.

9. Monitoring and Evaluation

After implementation, strategic minds monitor the outcomes of their decisions. They evaluate the results and adjust their approach if necessary to achieve the desired objectives.

10. Learning and Continuous Improvement

Rational decision-making involves learning from both successes and failures. Leaders use this knowledge to continuously improve their decision-making process.

Conclusion

Rational decision-making is a fundamental aspect of strategic minds, enabling leaders to make sound choices that drive organizational success. By following a structured and logical approach, leaders can navigate complexities, solve problems effectively, and seize opportunities with confidence. As we conclude our exploration of rational decision-making, let us recognize that this approach helps leaders maintain objectivity and make informed choices that align with their vision and values. By embracing rational decision-making, leaders can elevate their strategic thinking, inspire their teams, and achieve remarkable results that set their organizations on a path of sustainable growth and success.

2. Intuitive Decision Making

Intuitive decision-making relies on leaders' instincts and past experiences. Strategic leaders develop strong intuition through continuous learning and exposure to diverse situations, allowing them to make quick and informed decisions when faced with ambiguity.

Intuitive decision-making is a distinctive approach employed by strategic minds, allowing leaders to rely on their instincts and past experiences to make quick and informed choices. In this chapter, we explore the significance of intuitive decision-making in leadership and how it complements rational decision-making.

1. Understanding Intuitive Decision Making

Intuitive decision-making involves tapping into leaders' accumulated knowledge, experience, and subconscious thinking to arrive at a decision without a lengthy analytical process.

2. Developing Intuition

Strategic leaders develop intuition through continuous learning, exposure to diverse situations, and reflection on past experiences. Intuition grows stronger with time and exposure to various challenges.

3. Trusting Gut Feelings

Intuitive decision-making requires leaders to trust their gut feelings. They rely on their instincts to quickly assess a situation and choose the most appropriate course of action.

4. Rapid Decision Making

Intuitive decision-making allows leaders to make rapid decisions, particularly in situations where time is of the essence. Their intuition guides them to act swiftly and decisively.

5. Complementing Rational Analysis

Strategic minds use intuition to complement rational analysis. While rational decision-making relies on data and logic, intuition provides additional insights and perspectives.

6. Dealing with Ambiguity

Intuitive decision-making thrives in situations of ambiguity and uncertainty. Leaders use their intuition to navigate complexities when all the information is not readily available.

7. Pattern Recognition

Leaders with strong intuitive decision-making skills possess excellent pattern recognition abilities. They can recognize familiar patterns and apply previous experiences to new situations.

8. Instincts for People Management

Intuitive decision-making is particularly valuable in people management. Leaders can gauge the needs and emotions of their team members, fostering a positive and supportive work environment.

9. Emotional Intelligence

Intuitive decision-making is closely linked to emotional intelligence. Leaders with high emotional intelligence can better access their intuition and understand the emotions of others.

10. Learning and Refining Intuition

Strategic leaders continually learn and refine their intuition. They review past intuitive decisions to learn from successes and mistakes, strengthening their intuitive capabilities.

Conclusion

Intuitive decision-making is a unique facet of strategic minds, enabling leaders to make swift and well-informed choices based on their accumulated knowledge and experiences. By developing and trusting their intuition, leaders can complement rational decision-making and navigate uncertainties with confidence. As we conclude our exploration of intuitive decision-making, let us recognize that this approach is not a replacement for rational analysis but a valuable addition to a leader's toolkit. By leveraging intuitive decision-making, leaders can achieve agility, seize opportunities, and inspire their teams to navigate complexities with clarity and insight.

3. Data-Driven Decision Making

Data-driven decision-making involves using data analytics and insights to inform choices. Strategic leaders gather relevant data, analyze trends, and rely on evidence to make well-grounded decisions that drive organizational success.

Data-driven decision-making is a powerful approach used by strategic minds to make well-informed choices based on evidence and insights derived from data analysis. In this chapter, we explore the significance of data-driven decision-making in leadership and how it enhances strategic thinking.

1. Leveraging Data for Decision Making

Data-driven decision-making involves using relevant and reliable data to inform choices. Strategic leaders recognize the value of data as a strategic asset for driving organizational success.

2. Data Collection and Analysis

To make data-driven decisions, leaders collect and analyze data from various sources. They use data analytics tools and techniques to gain valuable insights into market trends, customer behavior, and organizational performance.

3. Identifying Key Performance Indicators (KPIs)

Strategic minds identify key performance indicators (KPIs) that align with their objectives. KPIs provide quantifiable metrics to measure progress and guide decision-making.

4. Evidence-Based Decision Making

Data-driven decisions are evidence-based, relying on factual information rather than assumptions or personal biases. Leaders seek objective evidence to support their choices.

5. Predictive Analytics

Data-driven decision-making may involve predictive analytics, where leaders use historical data to forecast future trends and potential outcomes, enabling proactive decision-making.

6. Real-Time Insights

Strategic leaders value real-time insights derived from data analysis. Timely information allows them to respond quickly to changing circumstances and capitalize on emerging opportunities.

7. Aiding Complex Problem-Solving

Data-driven decision-making aids leaders in solving complex problems. They leverage data to identify patterns, trends, and potential solutions that may not be apparent through traditional analysis.

8. Fact-Based Communication

Leaders who use data-driven decision-making communicate with facts and evidence, enhancing the credibility of their choices and fostering trust among stakeholders.

9. Risk Mitigation

Data-driven decisions often involve risk mitigation strategies. Leaders assess potential risks and make calculated choices to minimize negative outcomes.

10. Continuous Improvement Through Data

Strategic minds use data to drive continuous improvement. They analyze the results of their decisions, identify areas for enhancement, and refine their strategies accordingly.

Conclusion

Data-driven decision-making is a fundamental aspect of strategic minds, empowering leaders to make informed choices that drive organizational success. By leveraging data and insights, leaders can gain a competitive advantage, optimize performance, and respond effectively to dynamic market conditions. As we conclude our exploration of data-driven decision-making, let us recognize that data is a valuable resource that, when used strategically, enhances a leader's ability to make well-informed and impactful choices. By embracing data-driven decision-making, leaders can elevate their strategic thinking, inspire data-driven cultures, and achieve remarkable results that set their organizations on a path of sustainable growth and success.

4. Collaborative Decision Making

Strategic minds recognize the value of collaboration in decision-making. They involve key stakeholders and team members in the process, seeking diverse perspectives and collective wisdom to arrive at optimal solutions.

Collaborative decision-making is a powerful approach used by strategic minds to harness the collective intelligence and creativity of their teams. In this chapter, we explore the significance of collaborative decision-making in leadership and how it fosters a culture of innovation and teamwork.

1. Embracing Collective Intelligence

Collaborative decision-making involves seeking input and perspectives from team members and stakeholders. Strategic leaders recognize that diverse viewpoints enrich the decision-making process.

2. Inclusive and Participative

Leaders who embrace collaborative decision-making create an inclusive and participative environment. They encourage open communication and value contributions from all team members.

3. Leveraging Diverse Expertise

Collaborative decisions benefit from the diverse expertise and experiences of team members. Leaders leverage this diversity to arrive at well-rounded and innovative solutions.

4. Building Consensus

Strategic minds use collaborative decision-making to build consensus among team members. They facilitate discussions to find common ground and mutual agreement on the best course of action.

5. Active Listening

Leaders who practice collaborative decision-making are active listeners. They genuinely consider the ideas and feedback of their team members, fostering a culture of trust and respect.

6. Empowering Team Members

Collaborative decision-making empowers team members to take ownership and responsibility for the decisions made. Leaders trust their teams to contribute meaningfully to the process.

7. Conflict Resolution

In collaborative decision-making, leaders address conflicts constructively. They navigate differences of opinion and find solutions that align with the organization's goals.

8. Synergy and Innovation

Collaborative decision-making encourages synergy and innovation. By bringing diverse perspectives together, leaders can generate creative solutions that may not be apparent through individual efforts.

9. Team Building and Cohesion

Strategic leaders use collaborative decision-making as a team-building tool. Working together on decisions strengthens team cohesion and fosters a sense of collective purpose.

10. Continuous Learning and Improvement

Collaborative decision-making promotes continuous learning. Leaders and team members learn from each other's expertise and experiences, driving ongoing improvement.

Conclusion

Collaborative decision-making is a cornerstone of strategic minds, enabling leaders to harness the collective wisdom of their teams and stakeholders. By fostering an inclusive and participative decision-making process, leaders can inspire a culture of innovation, teamwork, and trust. As we conclude our exploration of collaborative decision-making, let us recognize that effective collaboration is not just about reaching a decision; it is about building strong teams, nurturing creativity, and achieving exceptional results together. By embracing collaborative decision-making, leaders can elevate their strategic thinking, unlock the full potential of their teams, and achieve remarkable outcomes that set their organizations apart as visionary leaders in a dynamic and competitive world.

5. Risk-Based Decision Making

Risk-based decision-making involves considering potential risks and rewards when evaluating alternatives. Strategic leaders assess the probability and impact of risks, making calculated choices that embrace innovation while mitigating potential negative outcomes.

Risk-based decision-making is a calculated approach used by strategic minds to assess potential risks and rewards before making choices. In this chapter, we explore the significance of risk-based decision-making in leadership and how it fosters prudent and informed decision-making.

1. Identifying and Assessing Risks

Risk-based decision-making involves identifying and assessing potential risks associated with each alternative. Strategic leaders carefully consider the probability and impact of risks on the organization.

2. Weighing Risks and Rewards

Leaders evaluate the risks and rewards of each option to make informed choices. They strike a balance between taking calculated risks and seeking opportunities for organizational growth.

3. Mitigation Strategies

In risk-based decision-making, leaders develop mitigation strategies to minimize potential negative outcomes. They plan for contingencies to address challenges that may arise.

4. Long-Term Implications

Strategic minds consider the long-term implications of their decisions on the organization. They assess how risks and rewards align with the organization's strategic objectives.

5. Navigating Uncertainty

Risk-based decision-making thrives in uncertain environments. Leaders use their judgment and analysis to navigate complexities and make choices with confidence.

6. Scenario Planning

Leaders engage in scenario planning to anticipate potential outcomes based on different risk scenarios. This approach enhances their ability to make informed choices under changing circumstances.

7. Ethical Considerations

Ethical considerations are integral to risk-based decision-making. Leaders evaluate risks not only from a financial perspective but also in alignment with the organization's ethical values.

8. Balancing Innovation and Prudence

Strategic leaders strike a balance between pursuing innovation and exercising prudence in risk-based decision-making. They encourage innovative thinking while managing potential risks responsibly.

9. Risk Tolerance and Organizational Culture

Risk-based decision-making is influenced by the organization's risk tolerance and culture. Leaders ensure that their choices align with the organization's appetite for risk.

10. Learning from Past Experiences

Strategic minds learn from past experiences and use these lessons to refine their risk-based decision-making. Analyzing successes and failures informs future choices.

Conclusion

Risk-based decision-making is a vital aspect of strategic minds, enabling leaders to make prudent and informed choices that consider potential risks and rewards. By adopting a systematic approach to risk assessment and mitigation, leaders can navigate uncertainties and make well-calculated decisions that align with their organization's long-term goals. As we conclude our exploration of risk-based decision-making, let us recognize that effective risk management is an essential element of strategic leadership. By incorporating risk-based decision-making into their approach, leaders can foster resilience, drive sustainable growth, and achieve remarkable results that position their organizations for success in a dynamic and unpredictable business landscape.

6. Ethical Decision Making

Ethical decision-making is a cornerstone of strategic minds. Leaders prioritize ethical considerations, ensuring their choices align with organizational values and contribute positively to all stakeholders.

Ethical decision-making is a fundamental aspect of strategic minds, guiding leaders to make principled choices that align with moral values and social responsibility. In this chapter, we explore the significance of ethical decision-making in leadership and how it fosters trust, integrity, and sustainable success.

1. Upholding Organizational Values

Ethical decision-making involves upholding the organization's core values. Strategic leaders ensure that their choices reflect the ethical principles that guide the organization.

2. Consideration of Stakeholder Impact

Leaders with ethical decision-making skills consider the impact of their choices on all stakeholders, including employees, customers, investors, and the broader community.

3. Balancing Conflicting Interests

Ethical decisions often involve balancing conflicting interests. Strategic minds seek solutions that respect the needs of all stakeholders and prioritize the common good.

4. Ethical Decision-Making Framework

Leaders use an ethical decision-making framework to guide their choices. This framework involves evaluating options based on moral principles, laws, and ethical standards.

5. Transparency and Accountability

Ethical decision-making emphasizes transparency and accountability. Leaders communicate their decisions openly and take responsibility for their actions.

6. Avoiding Unethical Practices

Strategic leaders steer clear of unethical practices, even when faced with external pressures. They prioritize integrity over short-term gains.

7. Ethical Leadership Role Modeling

Ethical decision-making is exemplified through ethical leadership role modeling. Leaders set an example for their teams, encouraging ethical conduct at all levels.

8. Ethics Training and Education

Leaders invest in ethics training and education for their teams. This empowers employees to understand ethical dilemmas and make ethical choices in their roles.

9. Ethical Conflict Resolution

Ethical decision-making involves addressing ethical conflicts promptly and constructively. Leaders navigate such conflicts with integrity and fairness.

10. Building a Culture of Ethics

Strategic minds work towards building a culture of ethics within their organizations. Ethical values permeate all aspects of the organization's operations and decision-making.

Conclusion

Ethical decision-making is a defining trait of strategic minds, guiding leaders to make choices that uphold moral values and foster a culture of integrity. By prioritizing ethics in decision-making, leaders build trust among stakeholders, enhance their organization's reputation, and create sustainable success. As we conclude our exploration of ethical decision-making, let us recognize that ethical leadership is not a single decision but a continuous commitment to doing what is right. By embracing ethical decision-making, leaders can elevate their influence, inspire ethical behavior in their teams, and achieve remarkable results that positively impact their organization and society at large.

7. Pragmatic Decision Making

Pragmatic decision-making focuses on practicality and feasibility. Strategic leaders balance ambitious goals with realistic expectations, making decisions that are achievable and aligned with available resources.

Pragmatic decision-making is a practical approach used by strategic minds to balance ambition with realism and make choices that are feasible and achievable. In this chapter, we explore the significance of pragmatic decision-making in leadership and how it fosters effective implementation and long-term success.

1. Setting Achievable Goals

Pragmatic decision-making involves setting goals that are achievable and realistic. Strategic leaders avoid setting overly ambitious targets that may not be feasible given the available resources and constraints.

2. Assessing Resource Availability

Leaders who practice pragmatic decision-making assess the availability of resources, including financial, human, and technological, before making choices. They align their decisions with the organization's capabilities.

3. Evaluating Cost-Benefit Analysis

Pragmatic minds perform a thorough cost-benefit analysis for each alternative. They weigh the potential benefits against the costs and risks to make well-informed choices.

4. Prioritizing Short-Term Wins and Long-Term Goals

Strategic leaders strike a balance between pursuing short-term wins and long-term strategic goals. They recognize the importance of achieving immediate successes to build momentum for larger objectives.

5. Adapting to Changing Circumstances

Pragmatic decision-making is adaptable to changing circumstances. Leaders reassess their choices when new information arises, ensuring their decisions remain relevant and effective.

6. Identifying Quick Wins

Leaders with pragmatic decision-making skills identify quick wins— small, achievable goals that deliver tangible benefits in a short period. These quick wins motivate and inspire their teams.

7. Managing Risk and Uncertainty

Pragmatic minds manage risk and uncertainty by taking measured steps and considering potential challenges. They plan contingencies to address unforeseen events.

8. Balancing Innovation and Practicality

Pragmatic decision-making balances innovation with practicality. Leaders foster a culture of creativity while ensuring that innovative ideas are viable and aligned with strategic objectives.

9. Utilizing Existing Strengths

Leaders leverage their organization's existing strengths and capabilities when making pragmatic choices. They capitalize on core competencies to drive success.

10. Learning from Failures

Pragmatic decision-making involves learning from failures and setbacks. Leaders use these experiences to refine their approach and improve future decision-making.

Conclusion

Pragmatic decision-making is a critical aspect of strategic minds, enabling leaders to make choices that are feasible, realistic, and aligned with available resources. By adopting a practical approach, leaders can ensure effective implementation and drive sustained success. As we conclude our exploration of pragmatic decision-making, let us recognize that pragmatism does not mean shying away from ambition or innovation. Rather, it is a strategic approach that combines ambition with realism to achieve meaningful and impactful results. By embracing pragmatic decision-making, leaders can elevate their strategic thinking, foster adaptability, and achieve remarkable outcomes that contribute to the long-term growth and success of their organizations.

8. Decision Trees and Scenario Analysis

Strategic minds employ decision trees and scenario analysis to visualize potential outcomes and their associated probabilities. These tools help leaders evaluate alternatives under various circumstances, enhancing decision-making accuracy.

Decision trees and scenario analysis are powerful tools used by strategic minds to visualize potential outcomes and inform complex decision-making. In this chapter, we explore the significance of decision trees and scenario analysis in leadership and how they enhance the decision-making process.

1. Understanding Decision Trees

Decision trees are visual representations of decisions and their potential consequences. Strategic leaders use decision trees to map out various choices and their corresponding outcomes, helping them identify the best course of action.

2. Assessing Probability and Impact

Decision trees allow leaders to assess the probability and impact of each potential outcome. By assigning probabilities to different scenarios, leaders can prioritize actions based on their likelihood of occurrence.

3. Identifying Decision Points

In decision trees, leaders identify critical decision points, where different choices lead to different branches of outcomes. This analysis helps leaders understand the potential consequences of each decision.

4. Analyzing Trade-Offs

Decision trees aid leaders in analyzing trade-offs between different alternatives. Leaders can compare the potential benefits and risks associated with each choice to make informed decisions.

5. Visualizing Complex Decisions

Strategic minds use decision trees to visualize complex decisions with multiple interconnected factors. The visual representation simplifies the decision-making process, making it easier to understand and communicate.

6. Incorporating Uncertainty

Decision trees accommodate uncertainty by considering multiple possible outcomes. Leaders can assess the impact of uncertain events and plan accordingly.

7. Scenario Analysis for Risk Management

Scenario analysis involves assessing various future scenarios based on different assumptions. Strategic leaders use this tool for risk management, evaluating potential outcomes under different circumstances.

8. Preparing for Contingencies

Scenario analysis helps leaders prepare for contingencies. By exploring multiple scenarios, they can develop contingency plans to respond effectively to various situations.

9. Enhancing Strategic Planning

Decision trees and scenario analysis enhance strategic planning. Leaders can identify potential challenges and opportunities, making their strategic plans more robust.

10. Supporting Long-Term Decision Making

Strategic minds use decision trees and scenario analysis to support long-term decision-making. They assess the sustainability and resilience of their choices under various possible futures.

Conclusion

Decision trees and scenario analysis are valuable tools for strategic minds, enabling leaders to make informed decisions in complex and uncertain environments. By visualizing potential outcomes and assessing probabilities, leaders can optimize their choices and plan for contingencies. As we conclude our exploration of decision trees and scenario analysis, let us recognize that these tools are not predictors of the future but valuable aids for informed decision-making. By leveraging decision trees and scenario analysis, leaders can elevate their strategic thinking, enhance risk management, and achieve remarkable outcomes that position their organizations for success in a dynamic and unpredictable business landscape.

9. Long-Term Impact Analysis

Strategic leaders consider the long-term impact of their decisions on the organization, stakeholders, and the environment. They prioritize sustainable solutions that create lasting value and positive contributions.

Long-term impact analysis is a critical approach used by strategic minds to evaluate the potential consequences of decisions over an extended period. In this chapter, we explore the significance of long-term impact analysis in leadership and how it fosters sustainable success and responsible decision-making.

1. Considering Future Consequences

Long-term impact analysis involves considering the future consequences of decisions made today. Leaders assess how choices may shape the organization's trajectory in the years to come.

2. Aligning with Strategic Objectives

Strategic leaders ensure that their decisions align with the organization's long-term strategic objectives. They assess how choices contribute to the overall vision and mission of the organization.

3. Identifying Long-Term Risks and Opportunities

Long-term impact analysis helps leaders identify potential long-term risks and opportunities associated with each decision. Leaders can plan strategies to capitalize on opportunities and mitigate risks.

4. Sustainability and Corporate Social Responsibility

Strategic minds prioritize sustainability and corporate social responsibility in long-term impact analysis. They assess decisions' environmental and societal implications.

5. Balancing Short-Term Wins and Long-Term Goals

Leaders balance short-term wins with long-term objectives in their decision-making. They avoid sacrificing long-term sustainability for immediate gains.

6. Forecasting Market and Industry Trends

Long-term impact analysis involves forecasting market and industry trends. Leaders use this insight to position their organizations for success in the future landscape.

7. Preparing for Technological Advancements

Leaders anticipate technological advancements in long-term impact analysis. They assess how emerging technologies may disrupt or enhance their business.

8. Considering Changing Customer Needs

Long-term impact analysis considers evolving customer needs and preferences. Leaders adjust their strategies to meet future customer demands.

9. Evaluating Organizational Resilience

Strategic minds assess organizational resilience in long-term impact analysis. They plan strategies to ensure the organization can withstand future challenges.

10. Continuous Adaptation and Improvement

Long-term impact analysis involves continuous adaptation and improvement. Leaders review and adjust their strategies to remain relevant and effective over time.

Conclusion

Long-term impact analysis is a crucial aspect of strategic minds, enabling leaders to make choices that create sustainable success and positive contributions to society. By considering future consequences and aligning decisions with strategic objectives, leaders can steer their organizations toward enduring success. As we conclude our exploration of long-term impact analysis, let us recognize that strategic leadership extends beyond immediate results, encompassing a commitment to creating lasting value for all stakeholders. By embracing long-term impact analysis, leaders can elevate their strategic thinking, foster responsible decision-making, and achieve remarkable outcomes that position their organizations as leaders in a dynamic and ever-changing world.

10. Reflection and Continuous Improvement

Strategic minds reflect on past decisions to learn and improve their decision-making process. They recognize that continuous improvement is essential for honing their strategic thinking and leadership capabilities.

Reflection and continuous improvement are essential practices embraced by strategic minds to learn from past experiences, refine decision-making processes, and drive ongoing growth. In this chapter, we explore the significance of reflection and continuous improvement in leadership and how they foster adaptability and innovation.

1. Learning from Successes and Failures

Strategic leaders reflect on both successes and failures to learn valuable lessons. They celebrate achievements and identify areas for improvement to avoid repeating past mistakes.

2. After-Action Reviews

After-action reviews are a part of reflection and continuous improvement. Leaders assess the outcomes of decisions and actions, identifying strengths and areas for enhancement.

3. Seeking Feedback

Leaders actively seek feedback from team members, stakeholders, and customers. They value diverse perspectives and use feedback to drive positive change.

4. Embracing a Growth Mindset

Strategic minds embrace a growth mindset, viewing challenges as opportunities to learn and improve. They continuously seek ways to develop their skills and knowledge.

5. Encouraging a Learning Culture

Leaders foster a learning culture within their organizations. They encourage employees to seek opportunities for professional development and skill enhancement.

6. Benchmarking and Best Practices

Continuous improvement involves benchmarking against industry best practices. Leaders use this information to identify areas where their organization can excel.

7. Experimentation and Innovation

Strategic leaders promote experimentation and innovation. They create an environment where calculated risks are encouraged to drive progress.

8. Iterative Decision Making

Leaders adopt an iterative approach to decision-making. They recognize that not all decisions will be perfect initially, and adjustments may be necessary based on feedback and results.

9. Strategic Planning Revisions

Continuous improvement informs strategic planning revisions. Leaders refine their strategies based on insights gained from reflection and analysis.

10. Building a Learning Organization

By prioritizing reflection and continuous improvement, leaders build learning organizations that adapt to change and excel in a dynamic environment.

Conclusion

Reflection and continuous improvement are vital elements of strategic minds, allowing leaders to grow, innovate, and steer their organizations toward ongoing success. By fostering a culture of learning and adaptability, leaders can enhance their decision-making processes and drive positive change. As we conclude our exploration of reflection and continuous improvement, let us recognize that strategic leadership is not a destination but a journey of constant growth and refinement. By embracing reflection and continuous improvement, leaders can elevate their strategic thinking, inspire their teams, and achieve remarkable outcomes that position their organizations as agile and forward-thinking leaders in their respective industries.

Chapter 4: Communication and Influencing Skills

Chapter 4 explores the critical role of communication and influencing skills in the arsenal of strategic minds. Effective communication is the backbone of successful leadership, enabling leaders to articulate their vision, inspire others, and drive change. In this chapter, we delve into various aspects of communication and influencing that contribute to effective leadership.

1. The Power of Effective Communication

Leaders recognize the power of effective communication in conveying ideas, building relationships, and fostering collaboration. They develop strong communication skills to inspire trust and confidence in their teams and stakeholders.

Effective communication is the cornerstone of successful leadership and a pivotal skill for strategic minds. In this chapter, we explore the profound impact of effective communication on leaders' ability to articulate their vision, inspire action, and foster a culture of collaboration and innovation.

1. Creating a Shared Vision

Strategic leaders use effective communication to create and communicate a shared vision that inspires and unites their teams. Through clear and compelling messages, they paint a vivid picture of the organization's future, rallying everyone around a common purpose.

2. Aligning Teams and Objectives

Effective communication aligns teams and individual objectives with the organization's overarching goals. Leaders convey how each person's contributions fit into the bigger picture, fostering a sense of purpose and commitment.

3. Inspiring Trust and Confidence

Leaders who communicate effectively inspire trust and confidence in their teams and stakeholders. Transparent and authentic communication builds credibility, fostering a positive and supportive work environment.

4. Navigating Challenges

In times of uncertainty and challenges, effective communication becomes even more critical. Strategic minds use clear and honest communication to address concerns, manage expectations, and navigate obstacles with resilience.

5. Fostering Collaboration and Innovation

Effective communication encourages open dialogue and fosters a culture of collaboration and innovation. Leaders create spaces for sharing ideas, encouraging creativity, and welcoming diverse perspectives.

6. Building Strong Relationships

Communication is the foundation of strong relationships. Strategic leaders prioritize active listening and empathetic communication, forging strong bonds with team members and stakeholders.

7. Responding to Feedback

Effective communication includes being receptive to feedback. Leaders actively seek and respond to feedback, showing that they value others' input and are open to continuous improvement.

8. Adapting Communication Styles

Strategic minds adapt their communication styles to different situations and audiences. Whether addressing the board, employees, or customers, leaders tailor their messages for maximum impact.

9. Overcoming Communication Barriers

Effective communicators identify and overcome communication barriers. They clarify misunderstandings, simplify complex concepts, and ensure their message is received as intended.

10. Celebrating Successes and Milestones

Strategic leaders use effective communication to celebrate successes and milestones, recognizing the efforts of their teams and reinforcing a culture of achievement.

Conclusion

The power of effective communication cannot be overstated. Strategic minds recognize its potential to inspire, align, and drive transformative change. By mastering effective communication, leaders can elevate their strategic thinking, engage their teams, and achieve remarkable outcomes that propel their organizations to new heights of success. As we conclude this chapter, let us recognize that communication is not a one-way process but a dynamic exchange that empowers leaders to connect, influence, and shape the future of their organizations and the lives of those they lead.

2. Clear and Concise Messaging

Strategic minds communicate with clarity and conciseness. They convey complex ideas in simple terms, ensuring their message is easily understood by all.

Clear and concise messaging is a foundational element of effective communication for strategic minds. In this chapter, we explore the significance of crafting clear and succinct messages that cut through complexity, engage audiences, and drive understanding and action.

1. Eliminating Ambiguity

Clear and concise messaging leaves no room for ambiguity. Strategic leaders ensure their messages are straightforward, free from jargon, and easily comprehensible by all.

2. Distilling Complex Ideas

Strategic minds excel at distilling complex ideas into simple and accessible language. They break down intricate concepts into bite-sized pieces, making them more digestible for their audience.

3. Crafting Compelling Elevator Pitches

Leaders develop compelling elevator pitches—short and impactful summaries of their ideas that can be delivered in the time it takes to ride an elevator. These pitches captivate attention and convey key points effectively.

4. Tailoring Messages to Different Audiences

Strategic leaders tailor their messages to suit the preferences and needs of different audiences. They adjust the level of technical detail and tone to ensure maximum relevance and resonance.

5. Avoiding Information Overload

Effective communicators understand the importance of brevity. They avoid overwhelming their audience with an excessive amount of information and focus on conveying the most critical points.

6. Using Visual Aids

Strategic minds use visual aids, such as charts, graphs, and infographics, to supplement their messaging. Visuals enhance understanding and retention of information.

7. Communicating with Impact

Clear and concise messaging leaves a lasting impact on the audience. Leaders carefully choose their words to evoke emotions, inspire action, and leave a memorable impression.

8. Verifying Understanding

Leaders verify their audience's understanding of the message by encouraging questions and seeking feedback. This practice ensures that their communication has been effectively received and interpreted.

9. Enhancing Decision-Making

Clear and concise messaging enhances decision-making. When leaders present information succinctly and logically, stakeholders can make informed choices efficiently.

10. Repeating Key Messages

Strategic minds know the power of repetition. They reinforce key messages through various channels to ensure that their vision and objectives remain at the forefront of their audience's minds.

Conclusion

Clear and concise messaging is a vital aspect of effective communication for strategic minds. By crafting messages that are easily understood, memorable, and impactful, leaders can inspire action, drive alignment, and foster a culture of transparency and trust. As we conclude this chapter, let us recognize that the art of clear and concise messaging is honed through practice and feedback. By continually refining their communication skills, leaders can elevate their strategic thinking, engage their teams, and achieve remarkable outcomes that propel their organizations toward success and significance.

3. Active Listening

Leaders practice active listening to understand the perspectives and concerns of others fully. By actively engaging with their team members and stakeholders, they build trust and demonstrate empathy.

Active listening is a foundational skill for strategic minds, enabling leaders to connect with others, understand diverse perspectives, and foster effective collaboration. In this chapter, we explore the significance of active listening in leadership and its transformative impact on communication and relationships.

1. Creating a Supportive Environment

Strategic leaders create a supportive environment for active listening. They encourage open dialogue, show genuine interest in others' viewpoints, and value diverse opinions.

2. Focused Attention

Active listening requires focused attention. Leaders give their full focus to the speaker, avoiding distractions and demonstrating respect for their time and ideas.

3. Suspending Judgment

Strategic minds suspend judgment while actively listening. They refrain from forming conclusions prematurely and remain open to new information.

4. Empathy and Understanding

Leaders practice empathy and seek to understand the emotions and perspectives of others. They put themselves in the speaker's shoes, fostering a deeper connection.

5. Encouraging Participation

Strategic leaders encourage participation and ensure all team members have an opportunity to speak. They create a safe space where individuals feel comfortable sharing their thoughts.

6. Asking Clarifying Questions

To demonstrate active listening, leaders ask clarifying questions. This approach ensures they fully comprehend the speaker's message and intent.

7. Reflective Responses

Leaders provide reflective responses to validate others' feelings and opinions. They paraphrase what they have heard to confirm understanding and show they are engaged.

8. Resolving Misunderstandings

Active listening helps leaders identify and address misunderstandings promptly. By seeking clarification, they prevent miscommunications and foster clear communication.

9. Leveraging Active Listening in Conflict Resolution

Strategic minds use active listening in conflict resolution. They create an open space for parties to express their concerns and work towards a mutually beneficial resolution.

10. Learning and Growth

Leaders view active listening as a tool for continuous learning and growth. By embracing diverse perspectives, they broaden their understanding and make more informed decisions.

Conclusion

Active listening is a pivotal skill for strategic minds, transforming communication and relationships within an organization. By actively engaging with others, leaders build trust, inspire loyalty, and nurture a culture of openness and collaboration. As we conclude this chapter, let us recognize that active listening is more than just hearing words; it involves genuine curiosity and empathy for others. By prioritizing active listening, leaders can elevate their strategic thinking, strengthen their influence, and achieve remarkable outcomes that empower their teams and lead their organizations to greater success.

4. Tailoring Communication Styles

Effective leaders adapt their communication styles to suit different audiences. They recognize that different individuals may require different approaches to be effectively influenced.

Tailoring communication styles is a crucial skill for strategic minds, allowing leaders to connect effectively with diverse audiences and build meaningful relationships. In this chapter, we explore the significance of adapting communication styles to suit different individuals and situations.

1. Recognizing Individual Preferences

Strategic leaders recognize that individuals have varying communication preferences. They observe and adapt their approach to resonate with each person's unique style.

2. Understanding Different Communication Styles

Leaders familiarize themselves with different communication styles, such as assertive, analytical, expressive, and amiable. This knowledge helps them tailor their messages appropriately.

3. Flexibility and Versatility

Tailoring communication styles requires flexibility and versatility. Leaders adjust their tone, pace, and language to accommodate the preferences of their audience.

4. Building Rapport

Strategic minds use tailored communication to build rapport with their teams and stakeholders. They establish a connection by speaking in ways that resonate with others.

5. Adapting to Cultural Differences

Leaders operating in diverse environments consider cultural differences in their communication. They adapt their style to align with cultural norms and values.

6. Considering the Context

Tailoring communication styles involves considering the context of the conversation. Leaders adjust their approach based on whether the discussion is formal or informal, one-on-one or in a group.

7. Customizing for Stakeholders

In dealing with various stakeholders, leaders customize their communication style to address their specific interests and concerns.

8. Leveraging Emotional Intelligence

Emotional intelligence plays a significant role in tailoring communication styles. Leaders empathize with others and adjust their approach to support the emotional needs of their audience.

9. Engaging and Motivating Teams

Tailored communication helps leaders engage and motivate their teams effectively. By understanding what resonates with each team member, they foster a sense of purpose and commitment.

10. Enhancing Collaborative Efforts

Leadership involves collaboration, and tailoring communication styles enhances collaborative efforts. By adapting their communication to suit team dynamics, leaders facilitate effective teamwork.

Conclusion

Tailoring communication styles is an indispensable skill for strategic minds, empowering leaders to connect authentically with their teams and stakeholders. By adjusting their approach based on individual preferences, cultural differences, and contextual factors, leaders can foster better understanding, trust, and collaboration. As we conclude this chapter, let us recognize that effective communication is a two-way street; leaders must also be receptive to others' preferred communication styles. By embracing tailored communication, leaders can elevate their strategic thinking, build stronger relationships, and achieve remarkable outcomes that unite their organization and propel it toward shared success.

5. Storytelling for Impact

Strategic minds use storytelling to make their messages memorable and impactful. Through compelling narratives, they engage emotions and connect with their audience on a deeper level.

Storytelling is a powerful tool used by strategic minds to captivate audiences, convey complex messages, and inspire action. In this chapter, we explore the significance of storytelling in leadership and how it enhances communication and influence.

1. Connecting Emotionally

Storytelling enables leaders to connect emotionally with their audience. Through compelling narratives, leaders evoke empathy, inspire enthusiasm, and foster a sense of shared purpose.

2. Making Messages Memorable

Stories make messages memorable. Strategic leaders use storytelling to convey key points in a way that resonates with their audience, making the information more memorable and impactful.

3. Illustrating Vision and Values

Storytelling brings the organization's vision and values to life. Leaders use stories to illustrate how the organization's mission and principles guide actions and decisions.

4. Relatability and Authenticity

Stories create a relatable and authentic context for communication. By sharing personal anecdotes or anecdotes from within the organization, leaders humanize their message.

5. Engaging Stakeholders

Storytelling engages stakeholders by drawing them into the narrative. Leaders involve their audience in the journey, making them feel like an essential part of the organization's story.

6. Communicating Change and Transformation

Leaders use storytelling to communicate change and transformation effectively. Stories help others understand the need for change, embrace it, and envision a better future.

7. Inspiring Innovation and Creativity

Strategic minds use stories to inspire innovation and creativity. They share tales of successful problem-solving and out-of-the-box thinking to encourage similar behavior.

8. Fostering Organizational Culture

Storytelling is a powerful means to reinforce and foster organizational culture. Leaders share stories that exemplify the organization's values, reinforcing cultural norms.

9. Communicating Complex Ideas

Stories simplify complex ideas, making them accessible to a broader audience. Leaders use metaphors and analogies to explain intricate concepts in a relatable manner.

10. Influencing Decision-Making

Storytelling influences decision-making by appealing to emotions and rationality. Leaders craft stories that present facts and logic in a compelling narrative, guiding stakeholders toward favorable choices.

Conclusion

Storytelling is a hallmark of strategic minds, allowing leaders to communicate with impact, inspire, and influence positive change. By harnessing the power of storytelling, leaders can foster deeper connections, create lasting impressions, and drive meaningful action within their organizations. As we conclude this chapter, let us recognize that storytelling is an art that evolves with practice and experience. By honing their storytelling skills, leaders can elevate their strategic thinking, ignite the passion of their teams, and achieve remarkable outcomes that leave a lasting legacy for their organization and the people they serve.

6. Building Credibility and Trust

Leaders prioritize building credibility and trust through transparent and honest communication. They establish themselves as reliable sources of information and guidance.

Building credibility and trust is a fundamental aspect of effective leadership for strategic minds. In this chapter, we explore the significance of credibility and trust in leadership and how they form the bedrock of successful relationships and organizational success.

1. Demonstrating Competence

Strategic leaders build credibility by demonstrating competence in their roles. They showcase their knowledge, expertise, and ability to make informed decisions.

2. Acting with Integrity

Integrity is central to building trust. Leaders uphold ethical principles, act consistently with their values, and are transparent in their actions.

3. Fulfilling Commitments

Credible leaders fulfill their commitments and promises. They take responsibility for their words and actions, ensuring their actions align with what they have communicated.

4. Consistency in Behavior

Consistency in behavior fosters trust. Leaders exhibit a consistent demeanor, delivering a reliable and predictable experience for their teams and stakeholders.

5. Communicating Honestly and Transparently

Open and honest communication is essential for building trust. Leaders communicate openly, even when sharing difficult or uncomfortable information.

6. Valuing Feedback

Credible leaders value feedback and actively seek input from their teams and stakeholders. They use feedback to improve and demonstrate their receptiveness to others' perspectives.

7. Putting People First

Leaders who prioritize their people build trust with their teams. They show genuine care for their employees' well-being and growth.

8. Leading by Example

Strategic minds lead by example, reinforcing their credibility through their actions. They exemplify the behaviors and values they expect from others.

9. Admitting Mistakes and Learning from Failures

Credible leaders admit their mistakes and take responsibility for their failures. They view setbacks as learning opportunities and show resilience in bouncing back.

10. Empowering Others

Leaders who empower their teams earn trust and respect. They delegate responsibilities, give autonomy, and support their team members' growth and development.

Conclusion

Building credibility and trust is an ongoing endeavor for strategic minds. By acting with integrity, demonstrating competence, and valuing open communication, leaders can cultivate an environment of trust and collaboration. As we conclude this chapter, let us recognize that credibility and trust are earned through consistent actions and genuine interactions with others. By prioritizing trust-building efforts, leaders can elevate their strategic thinking, foster stronger relationships, and achieve remarkable outcomes that inspire loyalty and drive their organizations towards excellence.

7. Managing Difficult Conversations

Effective communicators skillfully manage difficult conversations. They approach challenging discussions with empathy and assertiveness, seeking resolutions that benefit all parties.

Managing difficult conversations is a critical skill for strategic minds, enabling leaders to address challenging issues, resolve conflicts, and foster constructive relationships. In this chapter, we explore the significance of effectively navigating difficult conversations in leadership.

1. Approaching with Empathy

Strategic leaders approach difficult conversations with empathy and compassion. They consider the emotions and perspectives of all parties involved.

2. Choosing the Right Time and Setting

Timing and setting are essential in managing difficult conversations. Leaders select an appropriate time and private, comfortable environment conducive to open dialogue.

3. Active Listening and Patience

Leaders practice active listening during difficult conversations. They patiently allow others to express themselves fully without interrupting.

4. Staying Calm and Composed

Staying calm and composed during difficult conversations sets a positive tone. Leaders manage their emotions to create a safe and respectful atmosphere.

5. Focusing on the Issue, Not the Person

Strategic minds focus on addressing the issue rather than blaming or criticizing the individual. They keep the conversation constructive and solution-oriented.

6. Asking Open-Ended Questions

Leaders use open-ended questions to encourage dialogue and gain deeper insights into the concerns and perspectives of others.

7. Finding Common Ground

Strategic leaders seek common ground during difficult conversations. They identify shared goals and interests to build a foundation for resolution.

8. Offering Constructive Feedback

When giving feedback, leaders ensure it is specific, actionable, and aimed at improvement rather than personal criticism.

9. Seeking Win-Win Solutions

Leaders strive for win-win solutions in difficult conversations, aiming to find resolutions that benefit all parties involved.

10. Following Up

Following up after difficult conversations demonstrates commitment to finding solutions. Leaders check on progress and offer support if needed.

Conclusion

Managing difficult conversations is an essential skill for strategic minds, enabling leaders to address challenges, resolve conflicts, and build stronger relationships. By approaching these conversations with empathy, patience, and a focus on constructive solutions, leaders can create an atmosphere of trust and collaboration. As we conclude this chapter, let us recognize that difficult conversations are opportunities for growth and understanding. By embracing them with a problem-solving mindset, leaders can elevate their strategic thinking, strengthen their influence, and achieve remarkable outcomes that cultivate a culture of open communication and continuous improvement within their organization.

8. Persuasive Communication

Strategic leaders employ persuasive communication techniques to influence others' opinions and actions positively. They use logic, data, and emotional appeals to garner support for their ideas.

Persuasive communication is a potent tool for strategic minds, enabling leaders to influence others' beliefs, attitudes, and behaviors positively. In this chapter, we explore the significance of persuasive communication in leadership and how it empowers leaders to drive change and achieve organizational goals.

1. Understanding the Audience

Strategic leaders begin with understanding their audience—their values, interests, and concerns. This knowledge helps them tailor their persuasive messages effectively.

2. Establishing Credibility

Persuasive communicators establish credibility by showcasing their expertise and track record of success. They position themselves as reliable sources of information and guidance.

3. Building Emotional Appeal

Persuasive communication includes emotional appeal. Leaders use storytelling, vivid language, and relatable anecdotes to evoke emotions and connect with their audience.

4. Presenting Compelling Evidence

Leaders back their arguments with compelling evidence and data. Facts and statistics reinforce their points and add credibility to their persuasive messages.

5. Addressing Counterarguments

Strategic minds anticipate and address potential counterarguments. By acknowledging opposing views and offering thoughtful responses, they strengthen their persuasive position.

6. Using Social Proof

Persuasive communicators use social proof to their advantage. They highlight success stories and endorsements to demonstrate that others support their ideas.

7. Leveraging Authority and Expertise

Leaders leverage their authority and expertise when persuading others. Their position as respected leaders adds weight to their persuasive messages.

8. Creating a Call to Action

Persuasive communication includes a clear call to action. Leaders inspire their audience to take specific steps aligned with their objectives.

9. Finding Common Ground

Leaders find common ground with their audience to foster a sense of shared goals and values. This shared understanding paves the way for persuasive influence.

10. Following Up and Reinforcing Messages

Following up and reinforcing persuasive messages is crucial for sustained impact. Leaders consistently emphasize key points and remind their audience of the benefits of taking action.

Conclusion

Persuasive communication is an indispensable skill for strategic minds, enabling leaders to inspire change and garner support for their vision. By understanding their audience, establishing credibility, and leveraging emotional appeal, leaders can drive meaningful transformation within their organizations. As we conclude this chapter, let us recognize that persuasive communication is an art that requires a delicate balance of logic and emotion. By mastering this skill, leaders can elevate their strategic thinking, gain buy-in for their initiatives, and achieve remarkable outcomes that position their organizations for continued growth and success.

9. Overcoming Resistance to Change

Leaders leverage their influencing skills to overcome resistance to change. They communicate the benefits of change and address concerns, inspiring their teams to embrace new directions.

Overcoming resistance to change is a critical challenge that strategic minds must address to drive successful transformations within organizations. In this chapter, we explore the significance of effectively managing resistance to change and strategies to navigate this complex terrain.

1. Communicating the "Why"

Leaders must communicate the rationale behind the proposed changes clearly. By explaining the purpose and benefits of the change, they create a compelling case for its necessity.

2. Addressing Concerns Empathetically

Strategic leaders empathize with those facing change and actively address their concerns. They listen attentively and acknowledge the emotional impact of change.

3. Involving Stakeholders

Involving stakeholders in the change process fosters ownership and reduces resistance. Leaders seek input from those affected by the change and incorporate their feedback.

4. Providing Support and Resources

Leaders support individuals through the change by providing the necessary resources, training, and guidance. This support instills confidence and helps ease the transition.

5. Celebrating Small Wins

Recognizing and celebrating small victories during the change process motivates individuals and reinforces positive progress.

6. Leading by Example

Strategic minds lead by example during times of change. They embrace the change themselves and model the desired behaviors for others.

7. Communicating a Clear Vision

Leaders communicate a clear and compelling vision for the future. A well-defined vision helps individuals understand the direction and purpose of the change.

8. Creating a Sense of Urgency

Leaders create a sense of urgency to motivate action and overcome complacency. Emphasizing the need for change propels individuals to support the transformation.

9. Anticipating and Managing Resistance

Strategic leaders anticipate potential resistance points and proactively address them. They develop contingency plans to manage challenges as they arise.

10. Fostering a Culture of Adaptability

A culture of adaptability supports change efforts. Leaders nurture an environment where continuous improvement and flexibility are valued and rewarded.

Conclusion

Overcoming resistance to change is a vital aspect of strategic leadership, allowing leaders to successfully navigate organizational transformations. By communicating effectively, providing support, and involving stakeholders, leaders can address resistance and foster a positive attitude towards change. As we conclude this chapter, let us recognize that change is a constant in today's dynamic world, and effective leaders embrace it as an opportunity for growth and innovation. By mastering the art of overcoming resistance to change, leaders can elevate their strategic thinking, lead their organizations through transformational journeys, and achieve remarkable outcomes that position their organizations for sustained success and relevance.

10. Leading by Example

In all aspects of communication and influencing, strategic minds lead by example. They embody the values and principles they communicate, setting a standard for their teams to follow.

Leading by example is a cornerstone of strategic leadership, enabling leaders to inspire, influence, and guide their teams effectively. In this chapter, we explore the significance of leading by example and how it shapes organizational culture and success.

1. Setting High Standards

Leaders who lead by example set high standards for themselves and their teams. They demonstrate excellence in their work and encourage others to strive for greatness.

2. Embodying Organizational Values

Strategic minds embody the organization's values in their actions and decisions. They act consistently with the principles they advocate.

3. Displaying Integrity and Ethics

Leaders uphold integrity and ethical conduct. They act honestly and ethically, earning the trust and respect of their teams and stakeholders.

4. Demonstrating Accountability

Leading by example includes taking accountability for successes and failures. Leaders take responsibility for their actions and decisions, setting a precedent for accountability within the organization.

5. Embracing Adaptability and Resilience

Strategic leaders demonstrate adaptability and resilience in the face of challenges. They approach change with a positive attitude, inspiring their teams to do the same.

6. Encouraging Collaboration and Teamwork

Leaders foster collaboration and teamwork by actively engaging with their teams. They encourage open communication and value diverse perspectives.

7. Prioritizing Work-Life Balance

Leading by example includes prioritizing work-life balance. Leaders demonstrate the importance of well-being by maintaining a healthy balance themselves.

8. Promoting Professional Development

Strategic minds value continuous learning and development. They invest in their own growth and encourage their teams to do the same.

9. Recognizing and Celebrating Achievements

Leaders celebrate the achievements of individuals and teams. Recognizing successes boosts morale and motivates others to perform at their best.

10. Communicating Openly and Transparently

Leading by example involves open and transparent communication. Leaders share information openly, fostering a culture of trust and open dialogue.

Conclusion

Leading by example is a hallmark of strategic leadership, shaping organizational culture and inspiring others to reach their full potential. By embodying values, demonstrating integrity, and promoting collaboration, leaders can create a positive and high-performing work environment. As we conclude this chapter, let us recognize that actions speak louder than words, and leaders who lead by example wield the greatest influence over their teams. By mastering the art of leading by example, leaders can elevate their strategic thinking, ignite passion and commitment in their teams, and achieve remarkable outcomes that position their organizations as beacons of excellence and success in their industries.

Chapter 5: Developing a Leadership Mindset

Chapter 5 delves into the importance of cultivating a leadership mindset for strategic minds. It explores the key attributes, beliefs, and habits that empower individuals to think and act like effective leaders.

1. Embracing Growth and Learning

Strategic leaders embrace a growth mindset, viewing challenges as opportunities for learning and improvement. They continuously seek knowledge and develop their skills to stay ahead in an ever-changing world.

Embracing growth and learning is a fundamental aspect of a leadership mindset for strategic minds. In this chapter, we explore the significance of continuous improvement and the pursuit of knowledge in developing effective leaders.

1. The Growth Mindset

A growth mindset is the foundation of embracing growth and learning. Leaders with this mindset believe that their abilities and intelligence can be developed through dedication and hard work.

2. Embracing Challenges

Leadership-minded individuals embrace challenges as opportunities for growth. They welcome new experiences that push them outside their comfort zones.

3. Learning from Failures

Strategic minds view failures as stepping stones to success. They analyze setbacks, extract valuable lessons, and use this knowledge to improve and evolve.

4. Seeking Feedback

Leaders who embrace growth actively seek feedback from peers, mentors, and team members. They use constructive criticism to identify areas for improvement.

5. Investing in Professional Development

Leaders prioritize their professional development by attending workshops, pursuing certifications, and seeking out learning opportunities.

6. Cultivating Curiosity

Leadership-minded individuals cultivate curiosity and a thirst for knowledge. They explore diverse topics and stay informed about industry trends and innovations.

7. Encouraging a Learning Culture

Strategic leaders foster a learning culture within their organization. They encourage employees to engage in continuous learning and provide resources to support their growth.

8. Mentoring and Coaching

Leaders with a growth mindset mentor and coach their team members. They actively support the development of others, nurturing their potential.

9. Setting Personal Goals

Leadership-minded individuals set personal goals for their growth and development. They track progress and celebrate achievements.

10. Leading by Example

Leaders who embrace growth and learning lead by example. They demonstrate their commitment to self-improvement, inspiring others to do the same.

Conclusion

Embracing growth and learning is a transformative aspect of a leadership mindset. By fostering a growth mindset, seeking feedback, and investing in continuous learning, leaders can cultivate a culture of innovation and excellence within their organizations. As we conclude this chapter, let us recognize that the journey of growth and learning is ongoing and boundless. By embracing a mindset of continuous improvement, strategic minds can elevate their thinking, inspire their teams, and achieve remarkable outcomes that position their organizations for sustained success in an ever-evolving world.

2. Taking Ownership and Initiative

Leaders with a leadership mindset take ownership of their actions and decisions. They proactively seek solutions and take initiative to drive positive change.

Taking ownership and initiative is a key element of the leadership mindset for strategic minds. In this chapter, we explore the significance of accountability and proactivity in effective leadership.

1. Personal Responsibility

Leadership-minded individuals take personal responsibility for their actions and decisions. They do not shy away from owning up to mistakes or acknowledging areas for improvement.

2. Accountability to the Team

Strategic leaders are accountable to their teams. They understand that their actions impact the success of the entire organization and work collaboratively to achieve shared goals.

3. Proactive Problem Solving

Leaders with a leadership mindset proactively address challenges and seek solutions. They anticipate potential issues and take action before problems escalate.

4. Seizing Opportunities

Leadership-minded individuals seize opportunities for growth and advancement. They do not wait for opportunities to come to them; instead, they actively pursue and create them.

5. Being Results-Oriented

Strategic minds prioritize results and outcomes. They set clear objectives and work diligently to achieve them, keeping the organization's vision in mind.

6. Initiative in Decision-Making

Leaders take initiative in decision-making. They analyze information, seek input when needed, and make timely and well-informed choices.

7. Embracing Challenges

Leadership-minded individuals embrace challenging situations with a positive outlook. They see obstacles as opportunities to demonstrate leadership and problem-solving skills.

8. Empowering Others

Leaders empower their teams by giving them autonomy and trust. They encourage team members to take ownership of their responsibilities and contribute to the organization's success.

9. Leading in Uncertainty

Leaders with a leadership mindset lead with confidence in times of uncertainty. They make decisions even when faced with limited information, recognizing that indecision can lead to stagnation.

10. Continuous Improvement

Leadership-minded individuals continuously seek ways to improve themselves and their teams. They never settle for the status quo and foster a culture of continuous improvement.

Conclusion

Taking ownership and initiative is a defining trait of a leadership mindset. By embracing personal responsibility, being proactive, and empowering others, leaders can create a culture of accountability and drive meaningful change within their organizations. As we conclude this chapter, let us recognize that leadership is not passive; it requires action and a willingness to take risks. By embodying ownership and initiative, strategic minds can elevate their thinking, inspire their teams, and achieve remarkable outcomes that position their organizations as leaders in their industries.

3. Fostering Resilience and Adaptability

A leadership mindset involves resilience and adaptability. Leaders view setbacks as temporary hurdles and bounce back stronger with lessons learned.

Fostering resilience and adaptability is an essential aspect of the leadership mindset for strategic minds. In this chapter, we explore the significance of resilience and adaptability in navigating challenges and leading through change.

1. Embracing Change

Leadership-minded individuals embrace change as a constant and necessary aspect of growth. They view change as an opportunity for improvement and innovation.

2. Bouncing Back from Setbacks

Strategic leaders demonstrate resilience in the face of setbacks. They quickly recover from failures, learning from them and using the experience to fuel future success.

3. Maintaining a Positive Outlook

Leaders with a leadership mindset maintain a positive outlook, even during challenging times. They inspire optimism within their teams and foster a sense of hope and possibility.

4. Cultivating Mental Toughness

Leadership-minded individuals cultivate mental toughness, allowing them to stay focused and composed under pressure.

5. Adaptability in Decision-Making

Strategic minds exhibit adaptability in decision-making. They are open to new information and adjust their choices based on changing circumstances.

6. Learning from Adversity

Leaders learn valuable lessons from adversity. They use challenges as opportunities for growth and personal development.

7. Encouraging Innovation

Leadership-minded individuals encourage innovation and creativity within their teams. They foster a culture where new ideas are welcomed and experimentation is encouraged.

8. Navigating Uncertainty

Leaders navigate uncertainty with confidence and composure. They make informed decisions, even when faced with limited information.

9. Flexibility in Leadership Style

Strategic leaders display flexibility in their leadership style. They adapt their approach to suit different situations and the needs of their team members.

10. Building Resilient Teams

Leaders with a leadership mindset build resilient teams. They provide support, resources, and encouragement to help their teams overcome challenges.

Conclusion

Fostering resilience and adaptability is an integral part of the leadership mindset. By embracing change, maintaining a positive outlook, and cultivating mental toughness, leaders can navigate challenges and lead their organizations through uncertain times. As we conclude this chapter, let us recognize that resilience and adaptability are not just individual traits; they are also essential qualities of successful organizations. By fostering resilience and adaptability within themselves and their teams, strategic minds can elevate their thinking, inspire their organizations, and achieve remarkable outcomes that position their organizations as agile and forward-thinking in an ever-changing world.

4. Developing Emotional Intelligence

Strategic minds develop emotional intelligence, understanding and managing their emotions and those of others. This skill enhances interpersonal relationships and decision-making.

Developing emotional intelligence is a vital component of the leadership mindset for strategic minds. In this chapter, we explore the significance of emotional intelligence in effective leadership and how it influences relationships and decision-making.

1. Self-Awareness

Leadership-minded individuals possess self-awareness, understanding their emotions, strengths, weaknesses, and how they impact others.

2. Managing Emotions

Strategic leaders effectively manage their emotions, staying composed and in control even in challenging situations.

3. Empathy and Understanding Others

Leaders with a leadership mindset exhibit empathy, understanding the emotions and perspectives of others. They build strong relationships based on genuine understanding.

4. Active Listening

Leadership-minded individuals practice active listening, fully engaging with others' perspectives and feelings to foster open communication.

5. Conflict Resolution

Strategic minds use emotional intelligence in conflict resolution. They approach conflicts with empathy and seek win-win solutions.

6. Inspiring and Motivating Others

Leaders with emotional intelligence inspire and motivate others by understanding and addressing their emotional needs.

7. Cultivating a Positive Work Environment

Leadership-minded individuals create a positive work environment by fostering emotional well-being and a sense of belonging among team members.

8. Handling Stress and Pressure

Strategic leaders effectively handle stress and pressure, maintaining their emotional balance and decision-making ability.

9. Social Skills and Relationship Building

Leaders with a leadership mindset excel in social skills, building meaningful relationships and networks within and outside their organizations.

10. Emotional Intelligence in Decision-Making

Emotional intelligence influences leaders' decision-making, allowing them to consider both rational and emotional factors.

Conclusion

Developing emotional intelligence is a transformative aspect of the leadership mindset. By nurturing self-awareness, empathy, and social skills, leaders can create a positive and productive work environment. As we conclude this chapter, let us recognize that emotional intelligence is a key differentiator in leadership success. By honing their emotional intelligence, strategic minds can elevate their thinking, strengthen their relationships, and achieve remarkable outcomes that foster a culture of emotional well-being and collaboration within their organizations.

5. Cultivating Empathy and Compassion

Leaders with a leadership mindset cultivate empathy and compassion. They understand the feelings and perspectives of others, creating a supportive and inclusive work environment.

Cultivating empathy and compassion is a core element of the leadership mindset for strategic minds. In this chapter, we explore the significance of empathy and compassion in effective leadership and how they foster a culture of understanding and support.

1. Understanding Others' Perspectives

Leadership-minded individuals cultivate empathy by seeking to understand others' perspectives and experiences. They put themselves in others' shoes to gain insights into their emotions and challenges.

2. Active Listening and Empathetic Communication

Strategic leaders practice active listening and empathetic communication to connect deeply with their teams. They create a safe space for open dialogue and validate others' feelings.

3. Supporting Well-Being

Leaders with a leadership mindset prioritize the well-being of their team members. They demonstrate compassion and offer support during both professional and personal challenges.

4. Recognizing Individuality

Leadership-minded individuals recognize the individuality of each team member. They appreciate diverse backgrounds and experiences, fostering a culture of inclusion.

5. Building Trust through Empathy

Empathy builds trust among team members and between leaders and their teams. Leaders who demonstrate empathy create a strong foundation for collaboration and mutual respect.

6. Emotional Support

Strategic leaders provide emotional support to their teams during difficult times. They offer encouragement and understanding, helping team members navigate challenges.

7. Appreciating Contributions

Leadership-minded individuals show appreciation for their team members' contributions. They acknowledge and celebrate achievements, reinforcing a positive and compassionate work environment.

8. Leading with Heart and Mind

Leaders lead with both their heart and mind, balancing empathy and compassion with strategic thinking and decision-making.

9. Resolving Conflicts with Empathy

Leaders use empathy to resolve conflicts effectively. They approach disagreements with compassion and seek to find resolutions that address the needs of all parties involved.

10. Inspiring Through Compassion

Leaders with a leadership mindset inspire their teams through compassion. They demonstrate care and concern, motivating their team members to perform at their best.

Conclusion

Cultivating empathy and compassion is a transformational aspect of the leadership mindset. By understanding others' perspectives, offering support, and demonstrating empathy, leaders can create a culture of compassion and unity within their organizations. As we conclude this chapter, let us recognize that empathy and compassion are powerful drivers of organizational success. By cultivating these qualities within themselves and their teams, strategic minds can elevate their thinking, strengthen their relationships, and achieve remarkable outcomes that foster a culture of empathy, understanding, and collaboration within their organizations.

6. Encouraging Innovation and Creativity

Leadership-minded individuals encourage innovation and creativity within themselves and their teams. They foster an atmosphere that values and rewards new ideas.

Encouraging innovation and creativity is a vital aspect of the leadership mindset for strategic minds. In this chapter, we explore the significance of fostering a culture of innovation and how it drives continuous improvement and organizational success.

1. Embracing a Growth Mindset

Leadership-minded individuals embrace a growth mindset, valuing the potential for innovation and improvement. They encourage their teams to view challenges as opportunities for creative solutions.

2. Creating a Safe Environment

Strategic leaders create a safe and supportive environment where team members feel comfortable expressing their ideas and taking risks.

3. Rewarding Creativity

Leadership-minded individuals recognize and reward creativity within their teams. They acknowledge innovative efforts and celebrate new ideas.

4. Encouraging Cross-Functional Collaboration

Strategic minds encourage cross-functional collaboration, bringing diverse perspectives together to spark creativity and problem-solving.

5. Providing Resources for Innovation

Leaders with a leadership mindset allocate resources and time for innovation projects. They invest in research and development to foster a culture of continuous improvement.

6. Inspiring by Example

Leadership-minded individuals inspire innovation by embracing creative approaches themselves. They lead by example, demonstrating the value of thinking outside the box.

7. Allowing for Experimentation

Strategic leaders allow room for experimentation and accept that failure is an inherent part of the innovation process.

8. Removing Barriers to Innovation

Leadership-minded individuals remove organizational barriers that hinder innovation. They streamline processes and encourage a flexible, adaptive culture.

9. Encouraging Curiosity and Exploration

Leaders foster curiosity and encourage their teams to explore new ideas, technologies, and methodologies.

10. Celebrating Successes

Leaders with a leadership mindset celebrate successful innovations, reinforcing the importance of creativity and motivating further innovative endeavors.

Conclusion

Encouraging innovation and creativity is a transformative aspect of the leadership mindset. By embracing a growth mindset, providing resources, and rewarding creativity, leaders can create a dynamic work environment that fosters innovation and continuous improvement. As we conclude this chapter, let us recognize that innovation is a powerful driver of organizational success and competitiveness. By cultivating a culture of innovation within their organizations, strategic minds can elevate their thinking, inspire their teams, and achieve remarkable outcomes that position their organizations at the forefront of their industries.

7. Practicing Self-Reflection

Leaders engage in regular self-reflection, analyzing their actions, strengths, and areas for growth. They use this self-awareness to continually improve as leaders.

Practicing self-reflection is a crucial component of the leadership mindset for strategic minds. In this chapter, we explore the significance of self-reflection and how it enhances personal growth and leadership effectiveness.

1. Evaluating Actions and Decisions

Leadership-minded individuals regularly evaluate their actions and decisions. They assess the outcomes and identify areas for improvement.

2. Recognizing Strengths and Weaknesses

Strategic leaders are aware of their strengths and weaknesses. They leverage their strengths and work on developing areas that need improvement.

3. Learning from Experiences

Leaders with a leadership mindset learn from their experiences, both successes and failures. They extract valuable lessons to inform their future actions.

4. Setting Personal Goals

Self-reflection helps leaders set personal goals for growth and development. They align these goals with their vision and aspirations.

5. Examining Leadership Style

Leadership-minded individuals examine their leadership style and its impact on their team members and organizational culture.

6. Seeking Feedback

Strategic leaders actively seek feedback from their teams, peers, and mentors. They use feedback to gain different perspectives and uncover blind spots.

7. Adapting to Changing Circumstances

Leaders practice self-reflection to adapt to changing circumstances and emerging challenges.

8. Cultivating Emotional Intelligence

Self-reflection enhances emotional intelligence, enabling leaders to understand and manage their emotions effectively.

9. Taking Responsibility for Growth

Leadership-minded individuals take responsibility for their personal growth and development. They proactively seek opportunities for learning and improvement.

10. Realigning with Purpose

Self-reflection helps leaders realign with their purpose and vision, ensuring their actions are in line with their long-term goals.

Conclusion

Practicing self-reflection is a transformative aspect of the leadership mindset. By evaluating actions, seeking feedback, and learning from experiences, leaders can continually improve and enhance their leadership effectiveness. As we conclude this chapter, let us recognize that self-reflection is a continuous journey of self-discovery and growth. By cultivating the habit of self-reflection, strategic minds can elevate their thinking, gain deeper insights into their leadership style, and achieve remarkable outcomes that position them as reflective, adaptive, and influential leaders within their organizations.

8. Building and Leading Effective Teams

A leadership mindset includes the ability to build and lead effective teams. Leaders identify and nurture talent, empowering their teams to achieve exceptional results.

Building and leading effective teams is a critical aspect of the leadership mindset for strategic minds. In this chapter, we explore the significance of teamwork and how effective leadership fosters collaboration and synergy.

1. Defining Clear Objectives

Leadership-minded individuals define clear objectives and communicate them to their teams. Clarity of purpose ensures everyone is aligned and working towards common goals.

2. Selecting the Right Team Members

Strategic leaders carefully select team members based on their skills, strengths, and alignment with the team's vision.

3. Creating a Positive Team Culture

Leaders foster a positive team culture built on trust, respect, and open communication. They promote camaraderie and collaboration among team members.

4. Encouraging Diversity and Inclusion

Leadership-minded individuals value diversity and inclusion, recognizing that a diverse team brings varied perspectives and fosters creativity.

5. Providing Support and Resources

Strategic leaders provide the necessary support and resources for their teams to succeed. They remove obstacles and offer guidance when needed.

6. Empowering Team Members

Leaders empower their team members by giving them autonomy and decision-making authority. They trust their team's capabilities and allow them to take ownership of their work.

7. Fostering Continuous Learning

Leadership-minded individuals foster a culture of continuous learning within their teams. They encourage professional development and offer learning opportunities.

8. Promoting Effective Communication

Effective team leadership requires promoting open, honest, and effective communication among team members.

9. Resolving Conflicts

Leaders address conflicts within their teams promptly and constructively. They facilitate dialogue and seek resolution while maintaining a positive team dynamic.

10. Recognizing and Celebrating Team Achievements

Leaders with a leadership mindset recognize and celebrate their team's achievements. They show appreciation for their efforts and contributions.

Conclusion

Building and leading effective teams is a transformative aspect of the leadership mindset. By defining clear objectives, fostering a positive team culture, and empowering team members, leaders can create high-performing teams that achieve remarkable results. As we conclude this chapter, let us recognize that effective team leadership is not just about managing tasks; it is about inspiring and guiding individuals to work together towards a common purpose. By developing the skills to build and lead effective teams, strategic minds can elevate their thinking, inspire collaboration, and achieve remarkable outcomes that position their organizations for sustained success and innovation.

9. Embracing a Visionary Outlook

Leadership-minded individuals embrace a visionary outlook. They think beyond short-term goals and envision a compelling future for their organization.

Embracing a visionary outlook is a fundamental element of the leadership mindset for strategic minds. In this chapter, we explore the significance of visionary thinking and how it drives organizational direction and long-term success.

1. Thinking Beyond the Present

Leadership-minded individuals think beyond the present and envision a compelling future for their organizations. They see possibilities and opportunities beyond current challenges.

2. Aligning with Core Values

Strategic leaders align their vision with their organization's core values. Their vision reflects the principles and purpose that guide their organization's actions.

3. Setting Ambitious Goals

Leaders with a visionary outlook set ambitious, yet achievable, goals that inspire and motivate their teams to strive for excellence.

4. Articulating the Vision

Leadership-minded individuals articulate their vision clearly and passionately, captivating their teams and stakeholders with the potential of their shared future.

5. Seeking Innovation and Disruption

Strategic leaders seek innovation and disruption in their industries. They challenge the status quo and lead their organizations to the forefront of change.

6. Creating a Roadmap for Success

Leaders with a visionary outlook create a roadmap for success, outlining the steps and strategies to achieve their vision.

7. Inspiring Action and Commitment

Leadership-minded individuals inspire action and commitment to the vision. They rally their teams around the shared purpose and values.

8. Adaptability in Pursuit of the Vision

Strategic leaders remain adaptable in their pursuit of the vision. They adjust their strategies as needed to respond to changing circumstances.

9. Envisioning Beyond Obstacles

Leaders with a visionary outlook envision beyond obstacles and setbacks, maintaining focus on their long-term objectives.

10. Sustaining the Vision

Leadership-minded individuals work tirelessly to sustain their vision. They ensure that the vision remains a guiding force in all aspects of their organization.

Conclusion
Embracing a visionary outlook is a transformational aspect of the leadership mindset. By thinking beyond the present, setting ambitious goals, and inspiring action, leaders can shape the future of their organizations. As we conclude this chapter, let us recognize that visionary thinking is not a passive dream; it is a powerful force that drives leaders to take bold actions and create lasting impact. By cultivating a visionary outlook, strategic minds can elevate their thinking, inspire their teams, and achieve remarkable outcomes that position their organizations as pioneers and leaders in their industries.

10. Inspiring and Motivating Others

Leaders with a leadership mindset inspire and motivate others to reach their potential. They communicate a compelling vision and ignite passion within their teams.

Inspiring and motivating others is a fundamental aspect of the leadership mindset for strategic minds. In this chapter, we explore the significance of leadership influence and how it empowers individuals to achieve their full potential.

1. Leading by Example

Leadership-minded individuals lead by example, demonstrating the values and behaviors they expect from their teams.

2. Communicating a Compelling Vision

Strategic leaders communicate a compelling vision that inspires and motivates their teams to work towards a shared purpose.

3. Recognizing and Celebrating Achievements

Leaders celebrate the achievements of their teams, reinforcing a culture of appreciation and recognition.

4. Providing Opportunities for Growth

Leadership-minded individuals provide opportunities for professional and personal growth, empowering their teams to reach new heights.

5. Offering Support and Encouragement

Strategic leaders offer support and encouragement to their teams during challenges, fostering resilience and perseverance.

6. Creating a Positive Work Environment

Leaders cultivate a positive work environment where team members feel valued and engaged.

7. Empowering and Delegating

Leadership-minded individuals empower their team members by delegating responsibilities and trusting their capabilities.

8. Providing Constructive Feedback

Strategic leaders provide constructive feedback to help their teams improve and grow.

9. Building Strong Relationships

Leaders build strong relationships with their teams based on trust, respect, and open communication.

10. Inspiring Purpose and Meaning

Leadership-minded individuals inspire a sense of purpose and meaning in their teams' work, connecting it to a greater impact.

Conclusion

Inspiring and motivating others is a transformational aspect of the leadership mindset. By leading by example, communicating a compelling vision, and providing support and encouragement, leaders can empower their teams to achieve remarkable results. As we conclude this chapter, let us recognize that leadership influence is a catalyst for positive change and growth. By inspiring and motivating others, strategic minds can elevate their thinking, ignite passion and commitment in their teams, and achieve remarkable outcomes that position their organizations for excellence and success.

Chapter 6: Ethics and Integrity in Leadership Thinking

Chapter 6 delves into the critical importance of ethics and integrity in the leadership mindset for strategic minds. It explores the significance of principled decision-making and the impact of ethical leadership on organizational success and trust.

1. Defining Ethical Leadership

Leadership-minded individuals understand the concept of ethical leadership and its role in guiding their actions and decisions.

Ethical leadership is a cornerstone of the leadership mindset for strategic minds. In this chapter, we explore the essence of ethical leadership and its profound impact on individuals, organizations, and society.

1. Upholding Moral Principles

Ethical leadership centers on upholding moral principles and values, guiding decision-making and actions with integrity and honesty.

2. Prioritizing the Greater Good

Leadership-minded individuals prioritize the greater good of all stakeholders, including employees, customers, partners, and the broader community.

3. Being Accountable and Responsible

Strategic leaders take accountability for their actions and decisions, recognizing the consequences and impact they may have.

4. Encouraging Ethical Conduct

Ethical leaders actively encourage ethical conduct within their teams and set a positive example for others to follow.

5. Balancing Long-Term and Short-Term Goals

Leadership-minded individuals balance long-term sustainability with short-term objectives, ensuring ethical practices align with organizational goals.

6. Transparency and Openness

Ethical leadership promotes transparency and open communication, fostering trust and confidence among team members and stakeholders.

7. Fairness and Equity

Strategic leaders demonstrate fairness and equity in their treatment of others, valuing diversity and inclusion within their organizations.

8. Ethical Decision-Making Process

Leadership-minded individuals engage in a deliberate and thoughtful ethical decision-making process, considering the implications of their choices on various stakeholders.

9. Building a Culture of Ethical Behavior

Ethical leadership fosters a culture of ethical behavior within an organization, where integrity is valued and rewarded.

10. Embodying Ethical Values

Ethical leaders embody ethical values, consistently aligning their behaviors with their principles and setting the standard for ethical conduct.

Conclusion

Defining ethical leadership is a transformative aspect of the leadership mindset. By upholding moral principles, promoting transparency, and fostering a culture of ethical behavior, leaders can create an organization with a solid foundation of trust and credibility. As we conclude this chapter, let us recognize that ethical leadership is not only an essential aspect of effective leadership, but it is also a reflection of an organization's character. By embracing ethical leadership in their thinking and actions, strategic minds can elevate their decision-making, inspire ethical conduct in others, and achieve remarkable outcomes that position their organizations as models of ethical excellence and social responsibility.

2. Upholding Organizational Values

Strategic leaders uphold the core values of their organization and act consistently with its principles.

Upholding organizational values is a critical element of the leadership mindset for strategic minds. In this chapter, we delve into the significance of aligning actions and decisions with the core values of the organization.

1. Understanding Organizational Values

Leadership-minded individuals thoroughly understand the core values that underpin their organization's culture and identity.

2. Leading by Example

Strategic leaders lead by example, demonstrating the organization's values through their behaviors and decisions.

3. Consistency in Actions

Leaders consistently align their actions with the organization's values, reinforcing the importance of these principles to their teams.

4. Integrating Values into Decision-Making

Leadership-minded individuals integrate organizational values into their decision-making process, ensuring that choices reflect the organization's mission and principles.

5. Communicating Values Clearly

Strategic leaders communicate the organization's values clearly to all stakeholders, fostering a shared understanding and commitment.

6. Reinforcing Values through Recognition

Leaders reinforce organizational values through recognition and rewards, acknowledging behaviors that exemplify these principles.

7. Addressing Misalignment

Leadership-minded individuals address any misalignment between actions and values promptly and take corrective measures.

8. Empowering Others to Uphold Values

Strategic leaders empower their team members to uphold organizational values, encouraging them to make decisions that align with the organization's principles.

9. Values as a Guide for Innovation

Leaders use organizational values as a guide for innovation, ensuring that new initiatives are congruent with the organization's vision and purpose.

10. Embodying Values in Organizational Culture

Leadership-minded individuals ensure that organizational values are deeply ingrained in the company culture, influencing how work is conducted and how teams collaborate.

Conclusion

Upholding organizational values is a transformative aspect of the leadership mindset. By leading by example, integrating values into decision-making, and reinforcing principles through recognition, leaders can create a cohesive and purpose-driven organization. As we conclude this chapter, let us recognize that organizational values are the compass that guides an organization's journey. By upholding these values in their leadership thinking and actions, strategic minds can elevate their decision-making, inspire a values-driven culture, and achieve remarkable outcomes that position their organizations as exemplars of ethical conduct and shared purpose.

3. Ethical Decision-Making

Leaders prioritize ethical decision-making, considering the moral implications of their choices on stakeholders and society.

Ethical decision-making is a fundamental aspect of the leadership mindset for strategic minds. In this chapter, we explore the significance of ethical considerations in the decision-making process.

1. Understanding Ethical Dilemmas

Leadership-minded individuals recognize ethical dilemmas that arise when decisions involve conflicting moral principles.

2. Evaluating Implications on Stakeholders

Strategic leaders evaluate the potential impact of their decisions on various stakeholders, considering their well-being and interests.

3. Applying Ethical Frameworks

Leaders use ethical frameworks and guidelines to analyze complex situations and arrive at principled decisions.

4. Seeking Input and Collaboration

Leadership-minded individuals seek input from diverse perspectives and collaborate with others to gain a comprehensive understanding of ethical implications.

5. Balancing Short-Term and Long-Term Effects

Strategic leaders consider the short-term and long-term effects of their decisions, avoiding actions that may compromise long-term sustainability.

6. Moral Courage and Accountability

Leaders demonstrate moral courage to make difficult ethical decisions and take responsibility for their choices.

7. Avoiding Unethical Rationalizations

Leadership-minded individuals are vigilant in avoiding rationalizations that could justify unethical conduct.

8. Ethical Decision-Making Training

Strategic leaders provide training and resources to help their teams navigate ethical decision-making challenges.

9. Ethical Audits and Reviews

Leaders regularly conduct ethical audits and reviews to assess the alignment of their decisions and actions with ethical principles.

10. Ethical Decision-Making as a Core Competency

Ethical decision-making becomes a core competency within the organization, guiding the behavior of all team members.

Conclusion

Ethical decision-making is a transformative aspect of the leadership mindset. By understanding ethical dilemmas, seeking collaboration, and applying ethical frameworks, leaders can make principled choices that serve the best interests of their stakeholders and society. As we conclude this chapter, let us recognize that ethical decision-making is not just a process; it is a reflection of an organization's commitment to integrity and responsibility. By embracing ethical decision-making in their leadership thinking, strategic minds can elevate their decision-making, inspire ethical behavior in their teams, and achieve remarkable outcomes that position their organizations as ethical leaders and stewards of trust and credibility.

4. Transparency and Openness

Leadership-minded individuals promote transparency and openness in their communication and actions.

Transparency and openness are essential elements of the leadership mindset for strategic minds. In this chapter, we explore the significance of fostering an environment of transparency and the positive impact it has on organizational culture and trust.

1. Communicating Freely and Honestly

Leadership-minded individuals communicate freely and honestly with their teams and stakeholders, sharing information openly.

2. Sharing Organizational Vision and Goals

Strategic leaders share the organization's vision and goals with clarity, ensuring alignment and understanding among all team members.

3. Discussing Challenges and Setbacks

Leaders openly discuss challenges and setbacks, encouraging a culture of learning and continuous improvement.

4. Encouraging Feedback and Input

Leadership-minded individuals actively seek feedback and input from their teams and stakeholders, valuing diverse perspectives.

5. Addressing Concerns and Questions

Strategic leaders promptly address concerns and questions raised by their teams, demonstrating responsiveness and respect.

6. Transparency in Decision-Making

Leaders practice transparency in their decision-making process, explaining the rationale behind choices to build trust.

7. Sharing Successes and Failures

Leadership-minded individuals openly share both successes and failures, fostering a culture of accountability and learning.

8. Reporting Performance and Results

Strategic leaders report organizational performance and results transparently, enabling informed decision-making at all levels.

9. Engaging in Open Dialogue

Leaders engage in open dialogue with their teams, promoting a collaborative and inclusive work environment.

10. Leading with Integrity and Authenticity

Leadership-minded individuals lead with integrity and authenticity, cultivating trust through consistent and transparent behavior.

Conclusion

Transparency and openness are transformational aspects of the leadership mindset. By communicating honestly, sharing vision and goals, and encouraging open dialogue, leaders can create a culture of trust and accountability within their organizations. As we conclude this chapter, let us recognize that transparency is a powerful catalyst for employee engagement and organizational success. By embracing transparency and openness in their leadership thinking and actions, strategic minds can elevate their decision-making, inspire open communication, and achieve remarkable outcomes that position their organizations as models of transparency and ethical leadership.

5. Encouraging Ethical Behavior

Strategic leaders encourage ethical behavior within their teams and hold themselves and others accountable.

Encouraging ethical behavior is a fundamental aspect of the leadership mindset for strategic minds. In this chapter, we explore the significance of fostering a culture of ethics and integrity within the organization.

1. Setting a Strong Example

Leadership-minded individuals set a strong example by consistently demonstrating ethical behavior in their actions and decisions.

2. Articulating Ethical Expectations

Strategic leaders clearly articulate ethical expectations and standards to their teams, leaving no room for ambiguity.

3. Incorporating Ethics into Values and Mission

Leaders integrate ethics into the organization's core values and mission, making ethical conduct an integral part of the organizational identity.

4. Rewarding Ethical Conduct

Leadership-minded individuals reward and recognize team members who exhibit ethical behavior, reinforcing its importance.

5. Providing Ethics Training and Resources

Strategic leaders provide ethics training and resources to help team members understand ethical challenges and navigate them effectively.

6. Creating Safe Channels for Reporting Ethical Concerns

Leaders establish safe and confidential channels for team members to report ethical concerns without fear of retaliation.

7. Addressing Ethical Violations Promptly

Leadership-minded individuals address ethical violations promptly and take appropriate actions to rectify the situation.

8. Promoting a Culture of Transparency

Leaders promote a culture of transparency, where ethical behavior is encouraged and unethical conduct is not tolerated.

9. Encouraging Ethical Decision-Making Collaboration

Strategic leaders encourage collaborative ethical decision-making, where team members can seek guidance and support from others.

10. Incorporating Ethics in Performance Evaluation

Leadership-minded individuals incorporate ethical behavior as a factor in performance evaluations, emphasizing its significance.

Conclusion

Encouraging ethical behavior is a transformative aspect of the leadership mindset. By setting a strong example, articulating ethical expectations, and rewarding ethical conduct, leaders can create an ethical culture that permeates all aspects of the organization. As we conclude this chapter, let us recognize that ethical behavior is the backbone of an organization's reputation and success. By embracing and encouraging ethical behavior in their leadership thinking and actions, strategic minds can elevate their decision-making, inspire integrity, and achieve remarkable outcomes that position their organizations as beacons of ethical excellence and trustworthiness in their industries.

6. Navigating Ethical Dilemmas

Leaders navigate ethical dilemmas with integrity and seek ethical solutions that align with their values.

Navigating ethical dilemmas is a crucial aspect of the leadership mindset for strategic minds. In this chapter, we explore the significance of addressing complex ethical challenges with integrity and ethical reasoning.

1. Recognizing Ethical Dilemmas

Leadership-minded individuals are adept at recognizing ethical dilemmas when they arise, acknowledging the complexity of moral decisions.

2. Seeking Different Perspectives

Strategic leaders seek different perspectives and consult with others to gain a comprehensive understanding of ethical dilemmas.

3. Understanding Consequences

Leaders thoroughly analyze the potential consequences of each possible course of action in an ethical dilemma.

4. Referring to Ethical Guidelines

Leadership-minded individuals refer to ethical guidelines, codes of conduct, and organizational values as a framework for decision-making.

5. Ethical Decision-Making Models

Strategic leaders utilize ethical decision-making models to guide them through the process of resolving ethical dilemmas.

6. Aligning with Core Values

Leaders align their decisions with the core values of the organization and their personal ethical beliefs.

7. Considering Stakeholder Perspectives

Leadership-minded individuals consider the perspectives and interests of all stakeholders affected by their decisions.

8. Balancing Short-Term and Long-Term Implications

Strategic leaders consider both short-term and long-term implications of their decisions in an ethical dilemma, prioritizing sustainability and societal impact.

9. Reflecting on Moral Principles

Leaders reflect on their moral principles and the ethical implications of their actions, seeking to act in accordance with their highest ethical standards.

10. Seeking Ethical Guidance

Leadership-minded individuals seek ethical guidance from mentors, advisors, or ethical committees when faced with particularly challenging ethical dilemmas.

Conclusion

Navigating ethical dilemmas is a transformative aspect of the leadership mindset. By recognizing ethical dilemmas, seeking different perspectives, and aligning decisions with ethical principles, leaders can make principled choices that reflect their values and benefit the greater good. As we conclude this chapter, let us recognize that navigating ethical dilemmas requires moral courage and a commitment to doing what is right. By embracing ethical reasoning in their leadership thinking and actions, strategic minds can elevate their decision-making, inspire ethical conduct, and achieve remarkable outcomes that position their organizations as ethical leaders and agents of positive change in the world.

7. Leading with Integrity

Leadership-minded individuals lead with integrity, earning the trust and respect of their teams and stakeholders.

Leading with integrity is a fundamental aspect of the leadership mindset for strategic minds. In this chapter, we explore the profound impact of leadership driven by honesty, authenticity, and moral principles.

1. Consistency in Actions and Words

Leadership-minded individuals demonstrate consistency between their actions and words, building trust and credibility with their teams.

2. Adhering to Ethical Principles

Strategic leaders adhere to ethical principles and values, even in challenging situations where ethical compromises may be tempting.

3. Honesty and Transparency

Leaders prioritize honesty and transparency in their communication, fostering an open and trustworthy work environment.

4. Taking Responsibility

Leadership-minded individuals take responsibility for their decisions and actions, acknowledging mistakes and learning from them.

5. Being Authentic and Genuine

Strategic leaders are authentic and genuine, embracing their unique qualities and showing vulnerability when appropriate.

6. Building a Culture of Integrity

Leaders build a culture of integrity within their organizations, where ethical behavior is the norm.

7. Respecting Others' Perspectives

Leadership-minded individuals respect others' perspectives and consider diverse viewpoints in their decision-making.

8. Being Accountable to Stakeholders

Strategic leaders are accountable to all stakeholders, valuing their interests and striving for the greater good.

9. Acting in the Best Interest of the Organization

Leaders act in the best interest of the organization, setting aside personal interests for the collective benefit.

10. Inspiring Ethical Conduct

Leadership-minded individuals inspire ethical conduct in their teams through their own example and guidance.

Conclusion

Leading with integrity is a transformational aspect of the leadership mindset. By being consistent, adhering to ethical principles, and inspiring ethical conduct, leaders can create a culture of trust and respect within their organizations. As we conclude this chapter, let us recognize that integrity is the foundation of leadership effectiveness and influence. By embracing integrity in their leadership thinking and actions, strategic minds can elevate their decision-making, inspire ethical behavior, and achieve remarkable outcomes that position them as true leaders of character and ethical excellence.

8. Fostering an Ethical Culture

Strategic leaders foster an ethical culture within their organizations, where ethical conduct is valued and rewarded.

Fostering an ethical culture is a pivotal aspect of the leadership mindset for strategic minds. In this chapter, we explore how leaders can create an environment where ethical behavior flourishes.

1. Leading by Example

Leadership-minded individuals lead by example, demonstrating ethical conduct in all aspects of their work.

2. Communicating Ethical Expectations

Strategic leaders communicate clear ethical expectations to their teams, making it a priority in the organizational culture.

3. Providing Ethical Training and Resources

Leaders offer ethical training and resources to equip their teams with the tools to navigate complex ethical challenges.

4. Establishing Ethical Guidelines

Leadership-minded individuals establish ethical guidelines and codes of conduct, providing a framework for decision-making.

5. Recognizing Ethical Role Models

Strategic leaders recognize and celebrate individuals who exemplify ethical behavior, reinforcing its importance in the organization.

6. Encouraging Ethical Decision-Making Collaboration

Leaders encourage collaborative ethical decision-making, promoting diverse perspectives and collective responsibility.

7. Creating Safe Reporting Channels

Leadership-minded individuals create safe and confidential channels for reporting ethical concerns, ensuring team members feel comfortable speaking up.

8. Addressing Ethical Issues Promptly

Leaders address ethical issues promptly and transparently, showing a commitment to resolving challenges with integrity.

9. Incorporating Ethics in Performance Evaluations

Strategic leaders incorporate ethical behavior as a criterion in performance evaluations, reinforcing its significance in the organization.

10. Emphasizing Long-Term Impact

Leadership-minded individuals emphasize the long-term impact of ethical conduct on the organization's reputation and success.

Conclusion

Fostering an ethical culture is a transformative aspect of the leadership mindset. By leading by example, communicating expectations, and encouraging ethical collaboration, leaders can create an environment where ethical behavior is valued and rewarded. As we conclude this chapter, let us recognize that an ethical culture is not simply a result of policies; it is a reflection of the collective values and beliefs of the organization. By fostering an ethical culture in their leadership thinking and actions, strategic minds can elevate their decision-making, inspire integrity, and achieve remarkable outcomes that position their organizations as beacons of ethical excellence and trusted partners in the marketplace.

9. Addressing Unethical Behavior

Leaders address unethical behavior promptly and take appropriate actions to maintain the organization's integrity.

Addressing unethical behavior is a critical aspect of the leadership mindset for strategic minds. In this chapter, we explore how leaders can respond effectively to maintain ethical standards and foster a culture of integrity.

1. Recognizing Unethical Behavior

Leadership-minded individuals are vigilant in recognizing signs of unethical behavior within their teams and organization.

2. Investigating Ethical Concerns

Strategic leaders conduct thorough and impartial investigations when ethical concerns are raised, ensuring a fair process.

3. Acting Promptly and Decisively

Leaders act promptly and decisively when addressing unethical behavior, preventing its escalation and negative impact.

4. Maintaining Confidentiality

Leadership-minded individuals maintain confidentiality during the investigation of ethical issues, protecting the privacy of all involved.

5. Applying Progressive Discipline

Strategic leaders apply progressive discipline as necessary, taking appropriate measures to correct unethical conduct.

6. Offering Support for Ethical Improvement

Leaders offer support and resources for team members to understand and improve their ethical decision-making.

7. Communicating Consequences

Leadership-minded individuals communicate the consequences of unethical behavior clearly, reinforcing the organization's commitment to integrity.

8. Encouraging Ethical Accountability

Strategic leaders encourage ethical accountability among all team members, empowering them to uphold ethical standards.

9. Setting a Standard of Transparency

Leaders set a standard of transparency when addressing unethical behavior, promoting an open and ethical organizational culture.

10. Learning from Ethical Incidents

Leadership-minded individuals use ethical incidents as opportunities for learning and improvement, strengthening the organization's ethical practices.

Conclusion

Addressing unethical behavior is a transformational aspect of the leadership mindset. By recognizing unethical conduct, acting promptly and transparently, and fostering ethical accountability, leaders can uphold the organization's integrity and create a culture of ethical excellence. As we conclude this chapter, let us recognize that addressing unethical behavior is not only about corrective action; it is about reinforcing the organization's commitment to ethical conduct. By addressing unethical behavior in their leadership thinking and actions, strategic minds can elevate their decision-making, inspire ethical behavior, and achieve remarkable outcomes that position their organizations as bastions of ethical leadership and responsible corporate citizenship.

10. Ethical Leadership in Times of Crisis

Leadership-minded individuals demonstrate ethical leadership during times of crisis, making decisions that prioritize the well-being of stakeholders.

Ethical leadership in times of crisis is a defining aspect of the leadership mindset for strategic minds. In this chapter, we explore the importance of upholding ethical principles and guiding organizations through challenging circumstances.

1. Prioritizing the Well-Being of Stakeholders

Leadership-minded individuals prioritize the well-being of stakeholders, including employees, customers, and the community, during times of crisis.

2. Communicating Transparently

Strategic leaders communicate transparently with all stakeholders, providing accurate information and updates about the crisis.

3. Making Decisions with Ethical Impact

Leaders consider the ethical impact of their decisions during a crisis, ensuring that choices align with organizational values and long-term sustainability.

4. Balancing Short-Term and Long-Term Objectives

Leadership-minded individuals strike a balance between short-term crisis management and long-term organizational goals.

5. Leading with Empathy and Compassion

Strategic leaders lead with empathy and compassion, understanding the emotional toll of the crisis on their teams and stakeholders.

6. Maintaining Ethical Standards

Leaders maintain ethical standards even in the face of pressure and uncertainty during a crisis.

7. Being Visible and Accessible

Leadership-minded individuals are visible and accessible to their teams and stakeholders, offering support and reassurance.

8. Demonstrating Flexibility

Strategic leaders demonstrate flexibility and adaptability, adjusting strategies as the crisis unfolds.

9. Collaborating with Stakeholders

Leaders collaborate with stakeholders, seeking collective solutions and support during the crisis.

10. Learning and Improving from Crisis Experiences

Leadership-minded individuals use crisis experiences as opportunities for learning and improvement, strengthening the organization's crisis preparedness and ethical response.

Conclusion

Ethical leadership in times of crisis is a defining moment for leaders. By prioritizing well-being, communicating transparently, and demonstrating empathy, leaders can navigate their organizations through difficult times while upholding ethical principles. As we conclude this chapter, let us recognize that ethical leadership during a crisis is a testament to a leader's character and values. By exemplifying ethical leadership in times of crisis through their thinking and actions, strategic minds can elevate their decision-making, inspire resilience, and achieve remarkable outcomes that position their organizations as ethical leaders and trusted partners in times of uncertainty.

Chapter 7: Leading Teams with a Strategic Mind

Chapter 7 explores the art of leading teams with a strategic mindset. It delves into the principles and practices that empower leaders to inspire collaboration, foster innovation, and achieve collective success.

1. Understanding the Dynamics of Effective Teams

Leadership-minded individuals understand the essential elements of effective teams, such as trust, clear communication, and shared goals.

Effective teams are the backbone of successful organizations. In this chapter, we explore the key dynamics that contribute to the effectiveness and cohesiveness of teams.

1. Shared Vision and Goals

Leadership-minded individuals foster a shared vision and common goals among team members, aligning everyone towards a unified purpose.

2. Trust and Psychological Safety

Strategic leaders build trust and psychological safety within their teams, creating an environment where team members feel comfortable taking risks and expressing their ideas.

3. Clear Roles and Responsibilities

Leaders ensure that each team member has clear roles and responsibilities, minimizing ambiguity and promoting accountability.

4. Open Communication

Leadership-minded individuals promote open and transparent communication within their teams, encouraging feedback and active listening.

5. Collaboration and Teamwork

Strategic leaders foster a culture of collaboration and teamwork, encouraging team members to support each other and work together towards shared objectives.

6. Conflict Resolution and Constructive Feedback

Leaders address conflicts within the team constructively and provide timely and constructive feedback to facilitate growth and improvement.

7. Diversity of Skills and Perspectives

Leadership-minded individuals recognize the value of diverse skills and perspectives within the team, enhancing problem-solving and creativity.

8. Continuous Learning and Development

Leaders prioritize continuous learning and development for team members, empowering them to grow both personally and professionally.

9. Celebrating Team Achievements

Strategic leaders celebrate team achievements and milestones, recognizing and appreciating the collective efforts that drive success.

10. Adaptability and Resilience

Leadership-minded individuals instill adaptability and resilience within their teams, enabling them to navigate challenges and seize opportunities effectively.

Conclusion

Understanding the dynamics of effective teams is a pivotal aspect of the leadership mindset. By fostering trust, open communication, and collaboration, leaders can create high-performing teams that contribute to the organization's success. As we conclude this chapter, let us recognize that effective teams are not merely a product of chance; they are cultivated through intentional leadership and nurturing. By understanding the dynamics of effective teams in their thinking and actions, strategic minds can elevate their decision-making, inspire teamwork, and achieve remarkable outcomes that position their organizations as magnets for top talent and collaborative achievement.

2. Aligning Team Objectives with Organizational Goals

Strategic leaders align team objectives with the overall organizational goals, ensuring everyone is working towards the same vision.

In this chapter, we explore the critical role of aligning team objectives with the broader organizational goals to ensure a unified and purpose-driven approach to achieving success.

1. Understanding Organizational Goals

Leadership-minded individuals thoroughly understand the overall goals and mission of the organization.

2. Communicating Organizational Goals to the Team

Strategic leaders effectively communicate organizational goals to their teams, ensuring clarity and shared understanding.

3. Breaking Down Goals into Achievable Objectives

Leaders break down larger organizational goals into smaller, achievable objectives for their teams.

4. Ensuring Relevance and Contribution

Leadership-minded individuals ensure that team objectives are directly relevant to the organization's goals and contribute to its success.

5. Establishing Key Performance Indicators (KPIs)

Strategic leaders set Key Performance Indicators (KPIs) to measure progress towards team objectives and overall organizational success.

6. Providing Resources and Support

Leaders provide the necessary resources and support to enable their teams to accomplish their objectives effectively.

7. Regularly Monitoring and Evaluating Progress

Leadership-minded individuals regularly monitor and evaluate team progress towards objectives, making adjustments as needed.

8. Celebrating Milestones and Achievements

Strategic leaders celebrate team milestones and achievements, reinforcing the importance of aligning team objectives with organizational goals.

9. Addressing Challenges and Roadblocks

Leaders address challenges and roadblocks that hinder the alignment of team objectives with organizational goals, finding creative solutions.

10. Encouraging Collaboration across Teams

Leadership-minded individuals encourage collaboration across teams to ensure that all departments work cohesively towards shared goals.

Conclusion

Aligning team objectives with organizational goals is a transformative aspect of the leadership mindset. By communicating effectively, providing support, and celebrating achievements, leaders can foster a sense of purpose and drive within their teams. As we conclude this chapter, let us recognize that alignment is the key to unlocking the full potential of the organization. By aligning team objectives with organizational goals in their thinking and actions, strategic minds can elevate their decision-making, inspire collective effort, and achieve remarkable outcomes that position their organizations as unified and high-performing entities in pursuit of a shared vision.

3. Creating a Culture of Collaboration

Leaders foster a culture of collaboration, where team members share ideas, support each other, and work together harmoniously.

In this chapter, we explore the vital role of leaders in cultivating a culture of collaboration within their teams and organizations, fostering an environment where teamwork thrives.

1. Emphasizing the Value of Collaboration

Leadership-minded individuals emphasize the value of collaboration and its positive impact on team performance and organizational success.

2. Promoting Open Communication

Strategic leaders promote open communication, encouraging team members to share ideas, feedback, and concerns freely.

3. Building Trust and Psychological Safety

Leaders prioritize building trust and psychological safety within the team, allowing members to express themselves without fear of judgment.

4. Recognizing and Rewarding Collaboration

Leadership-minded individuals recognize and reward collaborative efforts, reinforcing the importance of working together towards shared goals.

5. Facilitating Cross-Functional Collaboration

Strategic leaders facilitate cross-functional collaboration, breaking down silos and promoting synergies between different departments.

6. Providing Collaborative Tools and Platforms

Leaders offer collaborative tools and platforms that enable seamless communication and knowledge-sharing among team members.

7. Encouraging Diversity of Thought

Leadership-minded individuals encourage diversity of thought and perspectives, fostering creative solutions and innovative thinking.

8. Leading by Example

Leaders lead by example, demonstrating collaborative behavior and teamwork in their interactions with others.

9. Creating Collaborative Opportunities

Strategic leaders create opportunities for team members to collaborate on projects and initiatives, enabling them to leverage their collective strengths.

10. Evaluating and Improving Collaborative Efforts

Leadership-minded individuals evaluate the effectiveness of collaborative efforts and continuously seek ways to improve and enhance teamwork.

Conclusion

Creating a culture of collaboration is a transformational aspect of the leadership mindset. By emphasizing collaboration's value, promoting open communication, and rewarding teamwork, leaders can nurture an environment where creativity and innovation flourish. As we conclude this chapter, let us recognize that collaboration is the foundation of organizational synergy and success. By fostering a culture of collaboration in their thinking and actions, strategic minds can elevate their decision-making, inspire collective effort, and achieve remarkable outcomes that position their organizations as thriving communities of collaboration and shared achievement.

4. Empowering Team Members

Leadership-minded individuals empower their team members, providing autonomy and opportunities for growth and development.

Empowering team members is a critical aspect of the leadership mindset. In this chapter, we explore the significance of providing autonomy and support to enable team members to reach their full potential.

1. Delegating Responsibilities

Leadership-minded individuals delegate responsibilities and tasks to team members based on their strengths and expertise.

2. Providing Autonomy and Decision-Making Authority

Strategic leaders provide team members with the autonomy and decision-making authority needed to take ownership of their work.

3. Encouraging Risk-Taking and Learning from Failure

Leaders encourage team members to take calculated risks and view failures as learning opportunities for growth and improvement.

4. Offering Professional Development Opportunities

Leadership-minded individuals provide professional development opportunities, enabling team members to enhance their skills and knowledge.

5. Recognizing and Utilizing Individual Strengths

Strategic leaders recognize and utilize the unique strengths of each team member, creating a well-rounded and high-performing team.

6. Being a Supportive Mentor

Leaders act as supportive mentors, guiding and nurturing team members to help them reach their full potential.

7. Providing Resources and Tools

Leadership-minded individuals ensure that team members have access to the necessary resources and tools to excel in their roles.

8. Promoting a Culture of Learning

Strategic leaders promote a culture of continuous learning within the team, encouraging curiosity and a thirst for knowledge.

9. Fostering a Growth Mindset

Leadership-minded individuals foster a growth mindset, where team members believe in their ability to improve and develop over time.

10. Celebrating Individual Achievements

Leaders celebrate individual achievements, recognizing and appreciating the contributions of each team member.

Conclusion

Empowering team members is a transformative aspect of the leadership mindset. By providing autonomy, recognizing individual strengths, and fostering a culture of learning, leaders can unleash the potential of their teams. As we conclude this chapter, let us recognize that empowering team members is not about micromanagement; it is about nurturing talent and instilling a sense of ownership. By empowering team members in their thinking and actions, strategic minds can elevate their decision-making, inspire individual growth, and achieve remarkable outcomes that position their organizations as hubs of talent and innovation, with each team member contributing to collective success.

5. Cultivating an Innovation Mindset

Strategic leaders encourage an innovation mindset within their teams, promoting creative thinking and problem-solving.

In this chapter, we explore the pivotal role of leaders in cultivating an innovation mindset within their teams and organizations, driving creativity and transformative thinking.

1. Encouraging Creativity and Exploration

Leadership-minded individuals encourage team members to explore new ideas and embrace creative approaches to problem-solving.

2. Creating a Safe Space for Innovation

Strategic leaders create a safe and supportive environment where team members feel empowered to share innovative ideas without fear of judgment.

3. Embracing a Continuous Improvement Culture

Leaders embrace a culture of continuous improvement, valuing incremental innovations and learning from failures.

4. Rewarding and Recognizing Innovation

Leadership-minded individuals reward and recognize innovative ideas and contributions, reinforcing their significance in the organization.

5. Providing Time and Resources for Innovation

Strategic leaders allocate dedicated time and resources for team members to work on innovative projects and initiatives.

6. Encouraging Interdisciplinary Collaboration

Leaders encourage interdisciplinary collaboration, bringing together diverse perspectives to spark innovation.

7. Supporting Risk-Taking

Leadership-minded individuals support calculated risk-taking, understanding that innovation requires some degree of uncertainty.

8. Promoting Openness to Change

Leaders promote openness to change within the team, encouraging flexibility and adaptability in response to new ideas.

9. Leading by Example in Innovation

Strategic leaders lead by example, actively engaging in innovative practices and showing their commitment to continuous improvement.

10. Measuring and Tracking Innovation Progress

Leadership-minded individuals measure and track the progress of innovation efforts, fostering accountability and learning from successes and setbacks.

Conclusion

Cultivating an innovation mindset is a transformational aspect of the leadership mindset. By encouraging creativity, providing resources, and celebrating innovation, leaders can foster a culture where groundbreaking ideas flourish. As we conclude this chapter, let us recognize that innovation is the driving force behind organizational growth and success. By cultivating an innovation mindset in their thinking and actions, strategic minds can elevate their decision-making, inspire creativity, and achieve remarkable outcomes that position their organizations as trailblazers in their industries, always at the forefront of progress and transformation.

6. Nurturing Diversity and Inclusion

Leaders prioritize diversity and inclusion, recognizing the value of different perspectives and backgrounds in team dynamics.

In this chapter, we explore the critical role of leaders in nurturing diversity and inclusion within their teams and organizations, fostering an environment where every individual feels valued and empowered.

1. Embracing Diversity as a Strength

Leadership-minded individuals embrace diversity as a strength, recognizing that diverse perspectives lead to more robust and innovative outcomes.

2. Creating an Inclusive Culture

Strategic leaders actively foster an inclusive culture where all team members feel respected and included in decision-making processes.

3. Ensuring Equal Opportunities

Leaders ensure equal opportunities for professional growth and development, regardless of individuals' backgrounds or identities.

4. Championing Diversity Initiatives

Leadership-minded individuals champion diversity initiatives within the organization, encouraging diversity at all levels.

5. Empowering Employee Resource Groups

Strategic leaders empower and support Employee Resource Groups (ERGs) to create a sense of community and advocate for diverse voices.

6. Providing Cultural Awareness Training

Leaders offer cultural awareness training to increase understanding and sensitivity towards different cultural norms and practices.

7. Encouraging Diverse Leadership

Leadership-minded individuals actively seek and promote diverse individuals for leadership positions, fostering representation at all levels.

8. Addressing Bias and Discrimination

Leaders address bias and discrimination promptly and firmly, promoting a culture of respect and fairness.

9. Listening and Valuing Feedback

Strategic leaders actively listen to feedback from team members regarding diversity and inclusion, valuing their perspectives.

10. Measuring and Tracking Progress

Leadership-minded individuals measure and track progress in diversity and inclusion initiatives, holding the organization accountable for achieving inclusive goals.

Conclusion

Nurturing diversity and inclusion is a transformative aspect of the leadership mindset. By embracing diversity, promoting inclusion, and addressing bias, leaders can create a workplace where every individual can thrive and contribute their unique strengths. As we conclude this chapter, let us recognize that diversity and inclusion are not just buzzwords; they are essential components of a successful and forward-thinking organization. By nurturing diversity and inclusion in their thinking and actions, strategic minds can elevate their decision-making, inspire collaboration among diverse perspectives, and achieve remarkable outcomes that position their organizations as beacons of equality and progress in their industries and beyond.

7. Effective Communication within Teams

Leadership-minded individuals ensure effective communication within their teams, fostering clarity and transparency.

Effective communication is the cornerstone of successful teamwork. In this chapter, we explore the importance of fostering open and clear communication within teams to drive collaboration and productivity.

1. Establishing Open Channels of Communication

Leadership-minded individuals establish open channels of communication, ensuring that team members can express their ideas and concerns freely.

2. Active Listening and Empathy

Strategic leaders practice active listening and empathy, making an effort to understand and validate team members' perspectives.

3. Setting Clear Expectations

Leaders set clear expectations for communication protocols, ensuring that team members understand how and when to communicate effectively.

4. Encouraging Two-Way Feedback

Leadership-minded individuals encourage two-way feedback, promoting a culture of constructive feedback and continuous improvement.

5. Utilizing the Right Communication Tools

Strategic leaders utilize the appropriate communication tools, ensuring that information is conveyed efficiently and effectively.

6. Clarifying Roles and Responsibilities

Leaders clarify roles and responsibilities within the team, avoiding miscommunication and overlap in tasks.

7. Tailoring Communication Styles

Leadership-minded individuals tailor their communication styles to suit individual team members' preferences and needs.

8. Regular Team Meetings and Check-Ins

Leaders conduct regular team meetings and check-ins to keep everyone informed and engaged.

9. Transparency in Decision-Making

Strategic leaders practice transparency in decision-making, sharing information and rationale behind choices that impact the team.

10. Resolving Conflicts through Communication

Leadership-minded individuals use communication as a tool to resolve conflicts and foster positive team dynamics.

Conclusion

Effective communication within teams is a transformational aspect of the leadership mindset. By establishing open channels, promoting active listening, and fostering transparent communication, leaders can build strong and cohesive teams. As we conclude this chapter, let us recognize that communication is the backbone of collaboration and collective success. By prioritizing effective communication in their thinking and actions, strategic minds can elevate their decision-making, inspire a culture of open dialogue, and achieve remarkable outcomes that position their teams as high-performing and closely connected units working towards shared goals.

8. Delegating and Leveraging Strengths

Strategic leaders delegate tasks based on team members' strengths, optimizing productivity and efficiency.

Effective delegation and leveraging team members' strengths are vital aspects of the leadership mindset. In this chapter, we explore how leaders can optimize team performance by assigning tasks strategically and recognizing individual strengths.

1. Identifying Individual Strengths

Leadership-minded individuals take the time to identify each team member's unique strengths, skills, and expertise.

2. Assigning Tasks Based on Strengths

Strategic leaders assign tasks and projects to team members based on their individual strengths, maximizing efficiency and performance.

3. Empowering Team Members through Delegation

Leaders empower team members through delegation, giving them ownership and autonomy over their assigned tasks.

4. Providing Clear Instructions and Expectations

Leadership-minded individuals provide clear instructions and expectations when delegating, ensuring that team members understand the scope of their responsibilities.

5. Encouraging Skill Development

Strategic leaders encourage skill development and growth by delegating tasks that challenge and stretch team members' abilities.

6. Monitoring Progress and Providing Support

Leaders monitor the progress of delegated tasks and provide necessary support and resources to ensure successful outcomes.

7. Recognizing and Celebrating Achievements

Leadership-minded individuals recognize and celebrate the achievements of team members who excel in their delegated roles.

8. Promoting Collaboration and Knowledge Sharing

Strategic leaders encourage collaboration and knowledge sharing among team members to leverage their combined strengths.

9. Offering Opportunities for Leadership Development

Leaders offer opportunities for team members to take on leadership roles, further developing their skills and potential.

10. Adjusting Delegation Strategies as Needed

Leadership-minded individuals are flexible in their delegation strategies, making adjustments as team dynamics and goals evolve.

Conclusion

Delegating and leveraging strengths are transformative aspects of the leadership mindset. By identifying individual strengths, providing clear instructions, and celebrating achievements, leaders can create a dynamic and high-performing team. As we conclude this chapter, let us recognize that effective delegation not only benefits the team but also fosters individual growth and development. By delegating and leveraging strengths in their thinking and actions, strategic minds can elevate their decision-making, inspire a culture of empowerment, and achieve remarkable outcomes that position their teams as collaborative and impactful forces within the organization.

9. Resolving Conflicts Constructively

Leaders address conflicts within their teams constructively, promoting healthy resolution and team cohesion.

Conflict is a natural part of teamwork, but effective leaders understand the importance of resolving conflicts constructively to maintain a harmonious and productive work environment. In this chapter, we explore strategies for managing conflicts within teams.

1. Addressing Conflicts Early

Leadership-minded individuals address conflicts as soon as they arise, preventing them from escalating and affecting team dynamics.

2. Promoting Open Communication

Strategic leaders promote open communication among team members to encourage the expression of concerns and grievances.

3. Understanding Root Causes

Leaders seek to understand the root causes of conflicts, allowing for more targeted and effective resolutions.

4. Encouraging Empathy and Active Listening

Leadership-minded individuals encourage empathy and active listening during conflict resolution, fostering understanding between conflicting parties.

5. Finding Win-Win Solutions

Strategic leaders seek win-win solutions that consider the interests of all parties involved in the conflict.

6. Mediating Conflict Discussions

Leaders mediate conflict discussions impartially, ensuring that all voices are heard and conflicts are resolved fairly.

7. Promoting Collaboration over Competition

Leadership-minded individuals promote a culture of collaboration over competition, reducing the likelihood of conflicts arising from competing interests.

8. Focusing on Facts and Behaviors

Strategic leaders focus on discussing specific facts and behaviors rather than personal attacks during conflict resolution.

9. Seeking Third-Party Support when Necessary

Leaders seek third-party support, such as HR professionals or team coaches, when conflicts are complex or difficult to resolve internally.

10. Learning from Conflicts

Leadership-minded individuals view conflicts as learning opportunities, identifying areas for improvement and growth within the team.

Conclusion

Resolving conflicts constructively is a transformative aspect of the leadership mindset. By addressing conflicts early, promoting open communication, and seeking win-win solutions, leaders can foster a positive and collaborative team environment. As we conclude this chapter, let us recognize that conflict resolution is not about avoiding disagreements but rather finding healthy ways to navigate them. By resolving conflicts constructively in their thinking and actions, strategic minds can elevate their decision-making, inspire a culture of understanding, and achieve remarkable outcomes that position their teams as resilient and cohesive units, capable of overcoming challenges and achieving shared goals.

10. Celebrating Team Achievements

Leadership-minded individuals celebrate team achievements, recognizing the collective efforts that drive success.

Celebrating team achievements is an essential aspect of the leadership mindset. In this chapter, we explore the significance of recognizing and appreciating the collective efforts of the team.

1. Acknowledging Milestones and Successes

Leadership-minded individuals acknowledge and celebrate significant milestones and successes achieved by the team.

2. Publicly Recognizing Team Contributions

Strategic leaders publicly recognize and appreciate team members' contributions, highlighting their valuable roles in the team's accomplishments.

3. Personalized and Sincere Appreciation

Leaders offer personalized and sincere appreciation to team members, showing gratitude for their hard work and dedication.

4. Sharing Success Stories

Leadership-minded individuals share success stories and achievements with the organization, inspiring pride and motivation.

5. Organizing Team Events and Celebrations

Strategic leaders organize team events and celebrations to commemorate achievements and build team camaraderie.

6. Rewarding Outstanding Performance

Leaders reward outstanding performance through incentives, bonuses, or other forms of recognition.

7. Encouraging Peer-to-Peer Recognition

Leadership-minded individuals encourage team members to recognize and celebrate each other's achievements, fostering a positive team culture.

8. Showcasing Achievements to Stakeholders

Leaders showcase team achievements to stakeholders, demonstrating the team's impact on the organization's success.

9. Celebrating Learning and Growth

Strategic leaders celebrate not only big achievements but also the learning and growth that occur throughout the team's journey.

10. Emphasizing the Team's Collective Impact

Leadership-minded individuals emphasize how the team's collective efforts contributed to the achievement, reinforcing the power of teamwork.

Conclusion

Celebrating team achievements is a transformative aspect of the leadership mindset. By acknowledging milestones, publicly recognizing contributions, and fostering a culture of appreciation, leaders can boost team morale and motivation. As we conclude this chapter, let us recognize that celebrating achievements is not just a formality; it is an essential part of nurturing a positive and high-performing team. By celebrating team achievements in their thinking and actions, strategic minds can elevate their decision-making, inspire a culture of pride, and achieve remarkable outcomes that position their teams as motivated and engaged units, always striving for excellence and success.

Chapter 8: Navigating Change and Uncertainty

In this chapter, we explore the critical role of leaders in guiding their teams through periods of change and uncertainty, fostering adaptability and resilience.

1. Embracing a Growth Mindset

Leadership-minded individuals embrace a growth mindset, viewing change and uncertainty as opportunities for learning and development.

In this chapter, we explore the transformative power of a growth mindset for both leaders and their teams. Embracing a growth mindset is essential in navigating change and fostering continuous improvement.

1. Understanding the Growth Mindset

Leadership-minded individuals understand that a growth mindset is the belief that abilities and intelligence can be developed through dedication and hard work.

2. Emphasizing Learning and Development

Strategic leaders emphasize the importance of learning and development for themselves and their team members.

3. Viewing Challenges as Opportunities

Leaders see challenges as opportunities for growth and improvement rather than as obstacles to success.

4. Encouraging Risk-Taking and Resilience

Leadership-minded individuals encourage team members to take calculated risks and be resilient in the face of setbacks.

5. Cultivating a Culture of Curiosity

Strategic leaders foster a culture of curiosity, where team members are encouraged to ask questions and seek knowledge.

6. Providing Feedback as a Path to Improvement

Leaders provide constructive feedback as a way to support team members' growth and development.

7. Acknowledging Effort and Persistence

Leadership-minded individuals acknowledge and celebrate the efforts and persistence of team members in their pursuit of goals.

8. Demonstrating Humility and Willingness to Learn

Leaders lead by example, demonstrating humility and a willingness to learn from others.

9. Creating Opportunities for Skill Building

Strategic leaders create opportunities for team members to build new skills and expand their knowledge.

10. Supporting Lifelong Learning

Leadership-minded individuals promote lifelong learning within their teams and organizations.

Conclusion

Embracing a growth mindset is a transformative aspect of the leadership mindset. By fostering a culture of learning and development, viewing challenges as opportunities, and providing support and feedback, leaders can inspire continuous improvement and adaptability within their teams. As we conclude this chapter, let us recognize that a growth mindset is a powerful tool in navigating change and fostering resilience. By embracing a growth mindset in their thinking and actions, strategic minds can elevate their decision-making, inspire a culture of growth, and achieve remarkable outcomes that position their teams as adaptable and resilient, capable of thriving in an ever-changing world.

2. Communicating Transparently about Change

Strategic leaders communicate openly and honestly with their teams about upcoming changes and the reasons behind them.

In this chapter, we delve into the critical role of transparent communication during times of change. Effective leaders understand the importance of keeping their teams informed and engaged throughout the change process.

1. Establishing Open Channels of Communication

Leadership-minded individuals establish open and transparent channels of communication to keep team members informed about upcoming changes.

2. Sharing the Vision and Rationale Behind Change

Strategic leaders communicate the organization's vision and the reasons behind the change, helping team members understand its significance.

3. Addressing Concerns and Questions

Leaders encourage team members to voice their concerns and ask questions about the change, providing honest and thoughtful answers.

4. Providing Regular Updates

Leadership-minded individuals provide regular updates about the progress of the change and any adjustments to the plan.

5. Acknowledging Challenges and Uncertainties

Strategic leaders acknowledge the challenges and uncertainties associated with the change, fostering a sense of empathy and understanding.

6. Listening to Feedback and Input

Leaders actively listen to team members' feedback and suggestions, incorporating valuable insights into the change process.

7. Involving the Team in Decision-Making

Leadership-minded individuals involve the team in decision-making where appropriate, empowering them to have a say in the change.

8. Offering Support and Resources

Strategic leaders offer support and resources to help team members navigate the change successfully.

9. Recognizing and Celebrating Progress

Leaders recognize and celebrate milestones and achievements related to the change, reinforcing positive outcomes.

10. Being Accessible and Approachable

Leadership-minded individuals remain accessible and approachable during times of change, creating an environment where team members feel comfortable sharing their thoughts.

Conclusion

Transparent communication about change is a transformative aspect of the leadership mindset. By establishing open channels, sharing the vision, and listening to feedback, leaders can foster trust and confidence within their teams during times of uncertainty. As we conclude this chapter, let us recognize that transparent communication is a cornerstone of effective change management. By communicating transparently about change in their thinking and actions, strategic minds can elevate their decision-making, inspire confidence, and achieve remarkable outcomes that position their teams as adaptable and united, ready to face any change with resilience and determination.

3. Providing Support during Transitions

Leaders offer support and resources to help team members navigate through transitions and adjust to new circumstances.

In this chapter, we explore the critical role of leaders in providing support and guidance to their teams during periods of transition. Effective leaders understand the importance of helping team members navigate change with confidence and reassurance.

1. Understanding Team Members' Needs

Leadership-minded individuals take the time to understand each team member's unique needs and concerns during transitions.

2. Offering Emotional Support

Strategic leaders provide emotional support to team members, acknowledging the challenges and uncertainties they may be facing.

3. Communicating Empathy and Understanding

Leaders communicate empathy and understanding, reassuring team members that their feelings and experiences are valid and acknowledged.

4. Addressing Individual Concerns

Leadership-minded individuals address individual concerns and anxieties related to the transition, providing personalized support.

5. Providing Training and Skill Development

Strategic leaders offer training and skill development opportunities to help team members adapt to new roles and responsibilities.

6. Encouraging Peer Support

Leaders encourage peer support and collaboration, creating a sense of camaraderie and unity during transitions.

7. Establishing Mentorship Programs

Leadership-minded individuals establish mentorship programs, pairing experienced team members with those who may need extra guidance.

8. Offering Flexibility and Work-Life Balance

Strategic leaders offer flexibility and support for achieving work-life balance during periods of transition.

9. Celebrating Small Wins and Progress

Leaders celebrate small wins and progress made during the transition, reinforcing a positive mindset.

10. Providing Clear Direction and Guidance

Leadership-minded individuals provide clear direction and guidance, ensuring that team members know what is expected of them during the transition.

Conclusion

Providing support during transitions is a transformative aspect of the leadership mindset. By understanding team members' needs, offering emotional support, and providing clear guidance, leaders can help their teams navigate change with confidence and resilience. As we conclude this chapter, let us recognize that support during transitions is essential for fostering a smooth and successful change process. By providing support during transitions in their thinking and actions, strategic minds can elevate their decision-making, inspire trust, and achieve remarkable outcomes that position their teams as adaptive and well-prepared for any change that comes their way.

4. Encouraging Flexibility and Adaptability

Leadership-minded individuals encourage team members to be flexible and adaptable, able to adjust their strategies and approaches as needed.

In this chapter, we explore the importance of fostering flexibility and adaptability within teams. Effective leaders understand that the ability to adapt to changing circumstances is crucial for success in today's dynamic world.

1. Emphasizing the Importance of Adaptability

Leadership-minded individuals emphasize the significance of adaptability as a core competency within the team.

2. Demonstrating Flexibility in Leadership

Strategic leaders lead by example, demonstrating flexibility in their own decision-making and approaches.

3. Encouraging a Growth Mindset

Leaders encourage a growth mindset, where team members believe in their capacity to learn and adapt.

4. Promoting Learning Opportunities

Leadership-minded individuals promote learning opportunities that enable team members to acquire new skills and knowledge.

5. Creating a Culture of Experimentation

Strategic leaders foster a culture where team members are encouraged to experiment and try new approaches.

6. Supporting Risk-Taking

Leaders support calculated risk-taking, empowering team members to explore innovative solutions.

7. Providing Resources for Adaptation

Leadership-minded individuals provide the necessary resources and tools to facilitate adaptation.

8. Celebrating Adaptability and Resilience

Leaders celebrate instances of adaptability and resilience within the team, reinforcing its importance.

9. Addressing Fear of Change

Leaders address team members' fear of change and uncertainties, providing reassurance and guidance.

10. Recognizing Adaptability as a Strength

Leadership-minded individuals recognize adaptability as a strength during performance evaluations and team discussions.

Conclusion

Encouraging flexibility and adaptability is a transformative aspect of the leadership mindset. By emphasizing adaptability's importance, promoting a growth mindset, and supporting risk-taking, leaders can foster a dynamic and agile team. As we conclude this chapter, let us recognize that adaptability is a key factor in an organization's ability to navigate change and seize opportunities. By encouraging flexibility and adaptability in their thinking and actions, strategic minds can elevate their decision-making, inspire innovation, and achieve remarkable outcomes that position their teams as agile and resilient, always ready to embrace new challenges and excel in an ever-changing landscape.

5. Leading by Example in Times of Uncertainty

Strategic leaders lead by example during uncertain times, displaying composure and resolve in the face of challenges.

In this chapter, we explore the powerful impact of leaders who lead by example during times of uncertainty. Effective leaders understand that their actions and demeanor can significantly influence their teams' response to challenging situations.

1. Demonstrating Resilience and Composure

Leadership-minded individuals demonstrate resilience and composure, even in the face of uncertainty, inspiring confidence in their team members.

2. Maintaining Open and Transparent Communication

Strategic leaders maintain open and transparent communication, sharing information honestly and consistently with their teams.

3. Embracing a Positive Mindset

Leaders embrace a positive mindset, focusing on opportunities and solutions rather than dwelling on challenges.

4. Being Adaptable and Flexible

Leadership-minded individuals exhibit adaptability and flexibility, showing their team members the value of embracing change.

5. Acknowledging and Learning from Mistakes

Leaders acknowledge and learn from mistakes, setting a precedent for a growth-oriented and accountable team culture.

6. Seeking Input and Collaboration

Strategic leaders seek input from their team members and collaborate on decision-making, valuing diverse perspectives.

7. Balancing Confidence and Humility

Leadership-minded individuals balance confidence with humility, recognizing their strengths while remaining receptive to feedback and improvement.

8. Taking Care of Well-Being

Leaders prioritize their well-being and that of their team members, recognizing the importance of self-care during challenging times.

9. Displaying Empathy and Understanding

Strategic leaders display empathy and understanding towards their team members' emotions and concerns, showing genuine care.

10. Remaining Committed to Core Values

Leadership-minded individuals remain committed to the organization's core values, ensuring consistency in their actions and decisions.

Conclusion

Leading by example in times of uncertainty is a transformative aspect of the leadership mindset. By demonstrating resilience, embracing a positive mindset, and prioritizing transparent communication, leaders can inspire their teams to face challenges with strength and optimism. As we conclude this chapter, let us recognize that leadership by example is not just about talking the talk but also walking the walk. By leading by example in their thinking and actions, strategic minds can elevate their decision-making, inspire trust, and achieve remarkable outcomes that position their teams as confident and united, ready to tackle any uncertainty with courage and determination.

6. Maintaining Focus on Core Values and Goals

Leaders prioritize core values and organizational goals during periods of change, providing a sense of stability and direction.

In this chapter, we explore the importance of staying grounded in core values and goals during times of uncertainty. Effective leaders understand that a clear sense of purpose and direction is crucial for guiding their teams through challenges.

1. Reinforcing Core Values

Leadership-minded individuals consistently reinforce the organization's core values, emphasizing their significance in decision-making.

2. Aligning Actions with Values

Strategic leaders align their actions with the organization's core values, setting an example for their teams to follow.

3. Communicating the Mission and Vision

Leaders effectively communicate the organization's mission and vision, reminding their teams of the larger purpose they are working towards.

4. Prioritizing Strategic Goals

Leadership-minded individuals prioritize strategic goals, focusing their team's efforts on what truly matters.

5. Adapting Strategies, Not Values

Strategic leaders adapt strategies and approaches in response to uncertainty, but they remain steadfast in upholding core values.

6. Inspiring Commitment and Dedication

Leaders inspire commitment and dedication to the organization's mission, fostering a sense of shared purpose within their teams.

7. Recognizing Alignment with Values

Leadership-minded individuals recognize and celebrate instances where team members demonstrate alignment with core values.

8. Using Values as a Decision-Making Framework

Leaders use core values as a framework for making decisions, ensuring that choices are in line with the organization's principles.

9. Providing Stability in Turbulent Times

Strategic leaders provide stability and consistency by keeping the focus on core values and goals during uncertain periods.

10. Addressing Challenges with Values-Based Solutions

Leadership-minded individuals address challenges and obstacles with solutions that reflect the organization's core values.

Conclusion

Maintaining focus on core values and goals is a transformative aspect of the leadership mindset. By reinforcing values, aligning actions, and using them as a decision-making framework, leaders can guide their teams through uncertainty with clarity and purpose. As we conclude this chapter, let us recognize that core values and goals are the anchor that keeps the team grounded in the midst of uncertainty. By maintaining focus on core values and goals in their thinking and actions, strategic minds can elevate their decision-making, inspire dedication, and achieve remarkable outcomes that position their teams as purpose-driven and unwavering, always striving for excellence and staying true to their organizational identity.

7. Seeking Opportunities within Challenges

Leadership-minded individuals encourage their teams to view challenges as opportunities for growth and innovation.

In this chapter, we explore the transformative mindset of leaders who see challenges as opportunities for growth and innovation. Effective leaders understand that adversity can be a catalyst for positive change.

1. Embracing a Positive Perspective

Leadership-minded individuals embrace a positive perspective, reframing challenges as opportunities for learning and improvement.

2. Encouraging a Solution-Oriented Approach

Strategic leaders encourage their teams to adopt a solution-oriented approach when faced with challenges.

3. Promoting a Culture of Innovation

Leaders foster a culture of innovation, where team members are encouraged to think creatively and explore new ideas.

4. Learning from Setbacks
Leadership-minded individuals view setbacks as learning experiences, using them to improve future strategies.

5. Seeking Feedback and Input
Strategic leaders seek feedback and input from team members, valuing diverse perspectives to find innovative solutions.

6. Emphasizing Continuous Improvement
Leaders emphasize the importance of continuous improvement, encouraging their teams to seek opportunities for refinement.

7. Encouraging Risk-Taking
Leadership-minded individuals encourage calculated risk-taking, recognizing that taking bold steps can lead to significant breakthroughs.

8. Recognizing and Celebrating Innovations
Leaders recognize and celebrate innovative ideas and solutions, reinforcing the value of creative thinking.

9. Building Resilience through Challenges
Strategic leaders view challenges as opportunities to build resilience within their teams, preparing them for future endeavors.

10. Embodying Adaptability and Agility
Leadership-minded individuals embody adaptability and agility, demonstrating that change and challenges can be navigated successfully.

Conclusion
Seeking opportunities within challenges is a transformative aspect of the leadership mindset. By embracing a positive perspective, encouraging innovation, and fostering resilience, leaders can turn adversity into a stepping stone for growth and success. As we conclude this chapter, let us recognize that seeing challenges as opportunities is a powerful mindset that drives continuous improvement and innovation. By seeking opportunities within challenges in their thinking and actions,

strategic minds can elevate their decision-making, inspire creativity, and achieve remarkable outcomes that position their teams as forward-thinking and resourceful, always ready to turn obstacles into stepping stones towards greatness.

8. Creating a Safe Environment for Feedback

Strategic leaders create a safe and open environment for team members to share feedback and express concerns during uncertain times.

In this chapter, we explore the importance of fostering a safe and open environment for feedback within teams. Effective leaders understand that honest feedback is crucial for continuous improvement and growth.

1. Emphasizing the Value of Feedback

Leadership-minded individuals emphasize the value of feedback, showing that it is an essential aspect of personal and team development.

2. Welcoming Constructive Criticism

Strategic leaders welcome constructive criticism and view it as an opportunity to identify areas for improvement.

3. Providing Timely and Specific Feedback

Leaders provide timely and specific feedback to ensure that team members can act upon it effectively.

4. Encouraging Two-Way Communication

Leadership-minded individuals encourage two-way communication, creating a space where team members feel comfortable providing feedback to their leaders as well.

5. Practicing Active Listening

Strategic leaders practice active listening when receiving feedback, demonstrating that they value and respect their team members' opinions.

6. Offering Anonymous Feedback Options

Leaders offer anonymous feedback options to team members who may feel more comfortable providing input confidentially.

7. Using Feedback to Drive Improvement

Leadership-minded individuals use feedback as a driving force for improvement and innovation within the team.

8. Creating Feedback Guidelines

Leaders create guidelines for giving and receiving feedback to ensure that it is constructive and respectful.

9. Celebrating a Culture of Feedback

Strategic leaders celebrate and reward a culture of feedback, reinforcing its importance within the team.

10. Addressing Feedback Appropriately

Leadership-minded individuals address feedback promptly and take appropriate actions to address valid concerns.

Conclusion

Creating a safe environment for feedback is a transformative aspect of the leadership mindset. By valuing feedback, practicing active listening, and using it to drive improvement, leaders can foster a culture of continuous learning and growth. As we conclude this chapter, let us recognize that feedback is a valuable tool for enhancing team performance and strengthening relationships. By creating a safe environment for feedback in their thinking and actions, strategic minds can elevate their decision-making, inspire open communication, and achieve remarkable outcomes that position their teams as receptive and adaptable, always striving to be the best version of themselves.

9. Monitoring and Adapting to Change

Leaders continuously monitor the impact of change and adjust strategies accordingly to ensure success.

In this chapter, we explore the vital role of leaders in monitoring and adapting to change effectively. Effective leaders understand that staying vigilant and responsive are crucial for navigating uncertainty successfully.

1. Establishing Key Performance Indicators (KPIs)

Leadership-minded individuals establish relevant KPIs to measure the impact of change and track progress.

2. Regularly Assessing Progress

Strategic leaders regularly assess progress against KPIs and review the effectiveness of their strategies.

3. Staying Informed of External Factors

Leaders stay informed about external factors, such as market trends and competitor activities, to identify potential opportunities and challenges.

4. Encouraging Continuous Feedback

Leadership-minded individuals encourage continuous feedback from team members and stakeholders to gather insights for improvement.

5. Identifying Early Warning Signs

Strategic leaders identify early warning signs of potential issues or obstacles related to the change.

6. Flexibility in Decision-Making

Leaders demonstrate flexibility in decision-making, adapting their strategies as needed based on new information.

7. Seeking Expert Guidance

Leadership-minded individuals seek expert guidance or external perspectives when faced with complex challenges.

8. Involving the Team in Adaptation

Leaders involve their team in the adaptation process, fostering a collaborative approach to change management.

9. Leveraging Technology and Data

Strategic leaders leverage technology and data analytics to gain insights and support data-driven decision-making.

10. Embracing a Continuous Improvement Mindset

Leadership-minded individuals embrace a continuous improvement mindset, recognizing that change is an ongoing process.

Conclusion

Monitoring and adapting to change is a transformative aspect of the leadership mindset. By establishing KPIs, staying informed, and involving the team in adaptation, leaders can navigate change with agility and precision. As we conclude this chapter, let us recognize that change is inevitable, and effective leaders are vigilant in monitoring and responsive in adapting. By monitoring and adapting to change in their thinking and actions, strategic minds can elevate their decision-making, inspire a culture of resilience, and achieve remarkable outcomes that position their teams as adaptive and forward-thinking, ready to thrive in an ever-evolving landscape.

10. Celebrating Resilience and Success

Leadership-minded individuals celebrate the resilience and achievements of their teams during times of uncertainty.

In this final chapter, we explore the importance of celebrating resilience and success within teams. Effective leaders understand the significance of recognizing and appreciating their team members' efforts and achievements.

1. Acknowledging Resilience in the Face of Adversity

Leadership-minded individuals acknowledge and celebrate the resilience demonstrated by their team members during challenging times.

2. Recognizing Efforts and Progress

Strategic leaders recognize and appreciate the efforts made by their teams, regardless of the outcome, emphasizing the value of continuous improvement.

3. Celebrating Milestones and Achievements

Leaders celebrate significant milestones and achievements, fostering a sense of accomplishment and motivation within the team.

4. Providing Public Recognition

Leadership-minded individuals provide public recognition and praise to team members, showcasing their contributions to the organization's success.

5. Expressing Sincere Gratitude

Strategic leaders express sincere gratitude to their teams for their hard work and dedication.

6. Organizing Team Celebrations

Leaders organize team celebrations and events to commemorate successes and build team camaraderie.

7. Sharing Success Stories

Leadership-minded individuals share success stories and best practices within the team and throughout the organization.

8. Rewarding Outstanding Performance

Leaders reward outstanding performance with incentives, bonuses, or other forms of recognition.

9. Encouraging Peer Recognition

Strategic leaders encourage team members to recognize and celebrate each other's successes, fostering a positive team culture.

10. Cultivating a Culture of Celebration

Leadership-minded individuals cultivate a culture where celebrating resilience and success is an integral part of the team's DNA.

Conclusion

Celebrating resilience and success is a transformative aspect of the leadership mindset. By acknowledging efforts, recognizing achievements, and fostering a culture of celebration, leaders can uplift their teams and inspire continued excellence. As we conclude this book, let us recognize that celebrating resilience and success is not just a way to boost morale but also a powerful tool for sustaining a motivated and engaged team. By celebrating resilience and success in their thinking and actions, strategic minds can elevate their decision-making, inspire a culture of appreciation, and achieve remarkable outcomes that position their teams as empowered and united, always reaching new heights of achievement and collective success.

The significance of leadership thinking lies in its transformative impact on effective leadership.

Leadership thinking goes beyond traditional management practices and involves a strategic and forward-looking mindset that guides decision-making and actions. Here are key points reiterating its significance:

1. Vision and Direction: Leadership thinking allows leaders to envision a compelling future and set clear direction for their teams. By formulating a strategic vision, leaders inspire and align their team members towards common goals.

2. Adaptability and Resilience: Effective leadership requires the ability to navigate through uncertainty and change. Leadership thinking equips leaders with the agility to adapt to dynamic environments and bounce back from challenges with resilience.

3. Empowerment and Collaboration: Leadership thinking encourages leaders to empower their team members, fostering a collaborative culture that values diverse perspectives and contributions.

4. Ethical Decision-Making: Strategic minds prioritize ethical considerations, ensuring that decisions are not only effective but also morally sound, contributing to a positive organizational culture.

5. Continuous Improvement: Leadership thinking emphasizes a commitment to continuous improvement. Leaders with this mindset actively seek feedback, encourage innovation, and drive progress within their teams.

6. Transparent Communication: Effective leaders with leadership thinking communicate openly and transparently, fostering trust and buy-in from their team members. This facilitates a culture of open feedback and collaboration.

7. Emotional Intelligence: Strategic minds recognize the importance of emotional intelligence in leadership. They understand and manage their emotions and those of their team members, fostering stronger relationships and effective communication.

8. Opportunity Orientation: Leaders with leadership thinking see challenges as opportunities for growth and innovation, encouraging their teams to tackle obstacles with a positive and solution-oriented mindset.

9. Inspiring Others: Leadership thinking enables leaders to serve as role models, motivating and inspiring their teams to achieve greatness by embodying the qualities they seek in their team members.

10. Sustainable Success: By consistently applying leadership thinking, leaders can achieve sustainable success. Their ability to anticipate, adapt, and drive positive change creates a resilient organization that can thrive even in a rapidly changing world.

Overall, leadership thinking is the cornerstone of effective leadership, shaping leaders into visionary, empathetic, and agile decision-makers. Its impact reverberates throughout the organization, empowering teams, and creating a positive and innovative work environment. Leaders who embrace this mindset become catalysts for transformation, leading their teams to achieve exceptional outcomes and driving lasting success in their personal and professional endeavors.

Congratulations on completing "Leadership Thinking 101: The Art of Strategic Minds." Here are the key takeaways from this book to enhance your leadership journey:

1. Leadership Thinking: Embrace a strategic mindset that empowers you to envision a clear direction, adapt to challenges, and lead with resilience.

2. Core Elements of Strategic Minds: Develop visionary thinking, analytical skills, adaptability, risk management, and innovation to make well-informed decisions.

3. Effective Decision-Making: Employ rational, intuitive, data-driven, and collaborative approaches, considering ethical implications in your choices.

4. Communication and Influencing: Cultivate clear, empathetic, and persuasive communication to inspire collaboration and foster innovation.

5. Leadership Mindset: Foster a growth-oriented, emotionally intelligent, and innovative mindset to drive personal and team development.

6. Ethics and Integrity: Uphold ethical principles, transparency, and trust to build a strong and positive organizational culture.

7. Leading Effective Teams: Empower and nurture diversity within your team, promoting open communication, collaboration, and continuous improvement.

8. Navigating Change: Embrace change with resilience, focus on core values, and seize opportunities within challenges.

9. Creating a Feedback Culture: Establish a safe environment for open feedback, empowering your team members to contribute to continuous improvement.

10. Celebrating Resilience and Success: Recognize and celebrate the efforts and achievements of your team, fostering a motivated and engaged workforce.

Additional References for Further Exploration:

1. Book: "Good to Great" by Jim Collins - A classic book that explores the qualities of great companies and the principles of effective leadership.

2. Article: "The Neuroscience of Leadership" by David Rock and Jeffrey Schwartz - An insightful article on the relationship between neuroscience and leadership behaviors.

3. Podcast: "The Leadership Podcast" - A podcast featuring interviews and discussions with experts on leadership, communication, and decision-making.

4. TED Talk: "How Great Leaders Inspire Action" by Simon Sinek - A compelling talk on the power of Inspiring leadership and the concept of starting with "why."

5. Research Paper: "Emotional Intelligence and Effective Leadership" - A comprehensive study on the role of emotional intelligence in effective leadership.

Remember, leadership is a continuous journey of growth and learning. Stay curious, seek knowledge, and apply the principles of strategic thinking to lead with purpose and positive impact.

Thank you for joining us on this leadership exploration. Wishing you success and fulfillment in your leadership endeavors!

Mohd Arif

www.ingramcontent.com/pod-product-compliance
Lightning Source LLC
Chambersburg PA
CBHW070933260726
48661CB00003B/968